MAK
$4.95

D09455353

The Letters of
MATTHEW ARNOLD
TO ARTHUR HUGH CLOUGH

The Letters of
MATTHEW ARNOLD
TO ARTHUR HUGH CLOUGH

Edited with an
introductory study by
HOWARD FOSTER LOWRY

OXFORD
AT THE CLARENDON PRESS

Oxford University Press, Ely House, London W.1

GLASGOW   NEW YORK   TORONTO   MELBOURNE   WELLINGTON
CAPE TOWN   SALISBURY   IBADAN   NAIROBI   LUSAKA   ADDIS ABABA
BOMBAY   CALCUTTA   MADRAS   KARACHI   LAHORE   DACCA
KUALA LUMPUR   HONG KONG   TOKYO

FIRST PUBLISHED 1932
REPRINTED LITHOGRAPHICALLY IN GREAT BRITAIN
AT THE UNIVERSITY PRESS, OXFORD
BY VIVIAN RIDLER
PRINTER TO THE UNIVERSITY
1968

PREFACE

THIS book comes appropriately, I think, as the first publication in a study of Matthew Arnold and Arthur Hugh Clough that has now extended over several years.

Through the mediation of Professor Chauncey Brewster Tinker, of Yale University, I have had, and continue to enjoy, the full co-operation and assistance of the families of both the poets. Viscountess Sandhurst and Mrs. Frederick Whitridge have furthered my investigation of Matthew Arnold by placing at my disposal their father's books and papers. In like manner, Mr. Arthur H. Clough and Miss Blanche A. Clough have entrusted me with the entire collection of their father's manuscripts, journals, and correspondence, in which are included the letters from Arnold here printed. For another occasion I reserve the full account of my indebtedness, not merely for stores lavishly supplied, but also for hospitalities and friendships altogether delightful. It is but typical of the good offices I have been shown that I have been left entirely free to interpret documents as I wish and to form conclusions which become my whole responsibility.

Other members of the Arnold and Clough families have also helped me. Mrs. Arthur Clough has carefully collected and wisely put in order a chaotic mass of materials accumulated through the years. Mrs. Florence Vere O'Brien, Mrs. Eleanor Thwaites, and the Reverend Roger Wodehouse have been memorably kind. Mrs. Thwaites has aided me directly with the manuscript. Particularly from Professor Arnold Whitridge, of Columbia University, has come continued opening of new resources that I otherwise should not have found. He has seen to it that I lack nothing he can furnish. Moreover, I have had the benefit of his wide reading and of his critical insight.

I am glad, therefore, that these letters which may further commemorate the friendship celebrated in 'Thyrsis' shall appear first and stand alone. Many lovers of English poetry must have wondered about them and decided they were gone. Certainly I was surprised to encounter them. Clough's letters to Arnold, except for the one given here, have been destroyed. In January 1871, Arnold wrote his mother, 'I am troubled at having absolutely nothing of Clough's except his name in one or two books'.

As best I could, I have tried to construct a narrative. The first part of the introduction, which contains a good portion of new material, carries the story of the friendship to the point where the correspondence takes the theme. The second half of the introduction and the large amount of commentary and annotation are inevitable, it seems to me, because of the problem presented. Many of the letters had to be dated. The period in Arnold's life they cover is not too well known or represented by many documents of any kind. Information and proofs had to be pieced together from a variety of sources. What is more, Arnold often employs a kind of coterie-speech as baffling as it is amusing. And Clough's replies, often sorely needed, are lacking.

Even so, I shall perhaps seem to have ignored important matters. For example, a curiosity about 'Marguerite' distinguishes both the genuine student of nineteenth-century poetry and the genial gossip-monger. Were the stanzas from Switzerland addressed to a real person or do they represent, as Arnold said they did, a fiction? He never pretended, and I suppose few others have believed, that they were altogether uninspired. If I do not comment upon one or two letters which recall the poems to 'Marguerite', it is simply that I have nothing else to add. In books and papers where, by natural laws, I should have come upon the faint traces of *some* Blumine or Flower-Goddess, I have found nothing. To the history of Arnold's youthful fancies I can bring no enlightenment but what he himself here sets down.

The text is a literal one, except for the alteration of '&' to 'and'. The manuscripts of all the letters but two are now in possession of the Sterling Memorial Library at Yale, largely through the interest of certain members of the class of 1917, notably Mr. Henry E. Coe and Mr. Henry C. Taylor.

In another form this book was offered at Yale in partial fulfilment of the requirements for the degree of Doctor of Philosophy. Professor Tinker and I there began, he as the director of my work, an association to which he has contributed richly. He owns a library containing, among other things, an Arnold collection that is indispensable. To that collection this edition owes much. But it is of other obligations that I shall be for ever deeply conscious.

Professor Karl Young, in a graduate class at Yale, first pointed out to me, as he has to many others, the full significance of Arnold's life and work. At the time my investigations were begun, Professor Young was abroad, and he has since been burdened with appalling labours of his own. Nevertheless, he has continually volunteered and performed for me services too numerous to detail.

From Professor Waldo H. Dunn, of Wooster, I have had, as usual, complete aid and encouragement. He has given his time both to the manuscript and to the proof. Yet to me his kindness seems merely another incident in a friendship of many years.

I have enjoyed the full facilities of the British Museum, the Bodleian Library, the Bibliothèque Nationale, and the Library of the University of Michigan. My heaviest demands, however, have been laid upon the staff of the Yale University Library, particularly Miss Emily Hall, Miss Anne Pratt, and Mr. Donald Wing. Mr. Thomas Will Simpson and Mr. William McCarthy will recognize that this little book does not begin to contain the whole record of their good deeds, bestowed both in and out of hours.

For what is usually more than one reason, I am grateful

to the following: Professor George L. Hendrickson, of Yale; Professor James Holly Hanford, of Western Reserve University; Dr. Horatio Krans, Director of the American University Union at Paris; Mr. Roger Ingpen, and Mr. Alan Harris, of London; Mr. Owen E. Holloway, of Bristol; Mr. Charles Stevenson and Louise Destler Stevenson, of Cambridge; Mr. Bronson Winthrop, of New York City; Mr. Ralph Lowry, of Hartford; Mr. Kenneth Weihe, of New Haven; Miss Mildred Mendenhall, of Cleveland; Mrs. Helen Harrington Compton, of Washington, D.C.; Mr. Charles Stonehill, of New Haven; Mr. James H. Wishart, of Western Reserve University; and Mr. Richard Purdy, of Yale.

At Wooster I have cause to remember Professors Mary Rebecca Thayer, Gertrude Gingrich, Emeline McSweeney, Elizabeth Bechtel, William R. Westhafer, Frederick Wall Moore, John D. McKee, John T. Lister, Delbert G. Lean, George W. Bradford, Horace N. Mateer, and John W. Olthouse; Mr. Lowell Coolidge, Mr. Curt N. Taylor, Miss Irene Agricola, Miss Gretchen White, Miss Olla Fern Kieffer, Miss Roma Hobson, Mr. Robert Wills, Mr. Fred Mulhauser, Mr. William Harris, Mr. Harry T. Shamp, Mrs. Waldo H. Dunn, Miss Elma Sage, Miss Dorothy Thompson, Miss Elizabeth Miller, Mr. J. R. McLaughlin, and Mr. William Peery.

With Mr. Chilson Leonard, of Yale, who is completing a study of Arnold in America, as with Mr. Charles J. Hill and Ruth H. Hill, now at Smith College, I shall associate the memory of many gracious acts and many hours of good talk. Mr. Hill's generous treatment, extending over three years, I can hardly over-estimate. Mr. John F. Miller, of Pittsburgh, and Professor Wallace Notestein, of Yale, have also my gratitude. From both of them I have received counsel and encouragement, Professor Notestein's being all the more welcome because it continues the kindness I once invariably received from his father,

Dr. Jonas O. Notestein, late Professor of Latin in the College of Wooster.

To Dr. Charles F. Wishart, President of the College of Wooster, and to Mrs. Wishart, I owe here, as I have long owed in other ways, the sincerest appreciation I can express. To them, as to Dr. and Mrs. Elias Compton and to my mother, this book perhaps can seem a small token of my own affection.

To the Oxford University Press I extend thanks, not merely for the care given to this edition of the letters, but for the plan of other related publications. Dr. Milford and Dr. Chapman have made most helpful suggestions; and in Captain G. F. J. Cumberlege I have had a moving spirit and resource I shall not readily forget.

It is a pleasure finally to acknowledge my obligation to the trustees of the Sterling Fellowships of Yale University, whose grant has let me have much time abroad; to the trustees of the College of Wooster; and to the Department of English of Yale University.

My only regret is that these letters will not be read by one who would perhaps most have delighted in them. From the inception of my work, Mr. John Bailey, who has written well of Arnold, was deeply interested. Whenever I was in London I knew that he would bring some new suggestion to my task. No one had a surer sense of Matthew Arnold's worth or a more abiding care for him. I last saw Mr. Bailey on a summer afternoon in Kent when we talked for hours of these and many things. I told him then something of the letters and their content. In only a few months I heard that he was dead. I do not feel quite free to dedicate this book to any one. But I am sure that Matthew Arnold and Arthur Clough would willingly let it be a slight memorial to a rare and gifted critic who was also one of England's gentlemen.

H. F. L.

THE COLLEGE OF WOOSTER,
September 1, 1932.

CONTENTS

TWO INTRODUCTORY CHAPTERS

I

THE friendship between Matthew Arnold and Arthur Hugh Clough belongs to Oxford, although its beginning was at Rugby. Long before either knew the autumn walks of Bagley Wood or the quiet corners of the Cumnor Hills, they had known each other, and to good account. To Arthur Clough, who was almost four years the older, Matthew Arnold was the son of a great man. Dr. Arnold, on the other hand, as did all the rest at Rugby, looked to Clough, his favourite pupil, as the school's chief promise of future fame. Out of early memories the ground of friendship and respect was surely formed.

It was in the summer of 1829 that Arthur Clough came to Rugby with his brother Charles. He was then ten years old. His family had returned the previous October to America, where Arthur himself had spent most of his childhood. In England he was quite alone, until 1836 having no home wherein to spend his holidays. Uncles and kindly cousins, with whom he often visited, could hardly supply the lack for a boy whose nature was exceedingly sensitive and affectionate. His own brother remained at school only until 1831. Even after six years at Rugby, indeed, Clough confided to his friend Simpkinson, then at Cambridge, that he did not know which to think greater, 'the blessing of being under Arnold, or the curse of being without a home'.[1] He refers, as the burden of his young years, to his sense of 'never being accustomed to be among those who I was sure loved me'.[2]

To such a boy Rugby was in double trust, and meant supremely more than it did to those young ruffians who were there only to give their English homes some kind relief. His school was for Clough his life. 'I verily believe', he confessed after the sixth year there, 'my whole being is soaked through with the wishing and hoping and striving to do the school good, or rather to keep it up and hinder it

[1] *Prose Remains*, London and New York, 1888, p. 64.
[2] A. H. C. to Simpkinson, MS. letter, November 5, 1835.

from falling in this, I do think, very critical time, so that all my cares and affections, and conversation, thoughts, words, and deeds, look to that involuntarily. I am afraid you will be inclined to think this "cant"—but this however is true—.' [1] When young Matt Arnold, then in the upper fifth form at home, where he had just come from a school at Winchester, finally saw Arthur Clough go up to Balliol, he felt with the others there that Rugby was sending out a boy more peculiarly its own than perhaps any other who had gone forth.

In Arthur Clough's day Rugby was Dr. Arnold. To the homeless boy, in whose genius they believed, both the head master and his wife became virtually second parents. They took him into their house on many occasions, where he learned to love both them and their children. 'I first knew him', the younger Thomas Arnold recalls,[2] 'as a boy at Rugby School. He was in the School-house, my brother and I at that time living at home, and preparing for Winchester with a private tutor. He was, I think, not seldom in the private part of the house; for my mother, who marked his somewhat delicate health, conceived a great liking for him; and his gentleness, and that unwonted *humanity* of nature which made him unlike the ordinary schoolboy, caused him to be a welcome guest in her drawing-room.' The diaries of Clough's early days record some of these visits, both at Rugby and at Fox How, Dr. Arnold's home in the Lake Country; and they detail his earnest fears that he has been 'too coxy' in his talk with Mrs. Arnold, or that he has said too much or spoken too presumptuously with the Doctor, who often flattered him with consultations on the problems of the school. As late as the second week of the Lent Term of 1838 at Oxford, he enters in his meditations, 'Thank God for Arnold, and his kindness of which I am most unworthy indeed'.[3] When

---

[1] A. H. C. to Simpkinson, letter of January 18, 1836, *Prose Remains*, p. 68.

[2] Tom Arnold, Matthew's younger brother, also became Clough's close friend. See his reminiscence in *The Nineteenth Century*, xliii (1898), 105–16.

[3] All references to the journals are from private unpublished note-books and papers which may be designated as the 'Clough MSS.'

the Head Master has come to visit him one day in his study, he can hardly look at his Trigonometry; and if he reflects occasionally that there are subtle dangers in the fagging system, there is always 'so much to look up to in Arnold' as to be exciting.

This is hardly the place to try an estimate of Dr. Arnold and his effect upon English education. Misunderstood in his own day, disliked and loved with equal violence, he is still in our time the object of both eulogy and satire. To many modern tempers, lusting for free expression and impatient of inhibitions earthly or divine, there is something unpleasant and pitiable about this man who 'carried his sheep in his hand'. To them he will never be more than the pious Englishman who turned Tom Brown's fellows into first-rate prigs and made little boys grow old before their years. And, probably, to the rough skull-breaking set at Rugby, although he won them too, he was, even in his own time, the embodiment of Duty waiting with a birch in hand, haunting their doubtful dreams like a Hebrew prophet, and summoning upon their guilty heads the fiery wrath of God.

But there was another kind of boy at Rugby to whom Dr. Arnold was a hero. To Arthur Stanley, Clough, and their like, this vigorous man with the flashing eyes, barely past forty and in the full abundance of his powers, opened a new world. If he taught them the reality of evil, he showed them also the glory of righteousness and the thrill of high endeavour. If he let them be over-concerned about their fellows, he sent them forth with an ardent social passion, into an England wherein man was yet unkind to man. They had heard of his love of beauty, of his travels in strange lands, of his zest for the mountain lakes which were his home, and of his deep affection for his children. And on Sundays, when into the pulpit of the Chapel he brought them an added something of himself, they forgave him whatever had offended them during the week, as he suggested to them man's life as it might some day be. With all his confessed errors in judgement, he had the charm that arises from a really great passion; he 'stands out among schoolmasters because he brought the zeal of a Crusader into what the world persists in thinking a prosaic profession'.[1]

About one side of Dr. Arnold and his work at Rugby too little has been said. Merely because he was a pioneer in his notion that the building of character was a task for the public schools, that phase of his work has largely obscured all others. His best pupils saw something else. They caught from their head master, not merely a moral straightening, but also a large intellectual deliverance. For Dr. Arnold cared about a boy's mind as well as about his conscience. He opened at Rugby a wealth of classical and historical learning that had no trace of pedantry. To religious thought he brought the newest discoveries of the continental school and a large way of thinking that was wholly divorced from the narrow theology of England. Under his touch, the civilizations of Greece and Rome lived again.

Matthew Arnold, who was a keen judge in such matters, saw clearly this other side of his father. He wrote once to his mother that Dr. Arnold's 'greatness consists in his bringing such a torrent of freshness into English religion by placing history and politics in connexion with it'.[2] If, indeed, the son was later to wander between two worlds in his attempt toward some congenial form of faith, his father had no small part in the movement of mind that set him wandering. And in one of the most charming and typical bits he ever wrote, Matthew Arnold, after praising Mr. Long for making Marcus Aurelius not the mere hero of a Classical Dictionary, but a living person, finally adds, 'Why may not a son of Dr. Arnold say, what might naturally here be said by any other critic, that in this lively and fruitful way of considering the men and affairs of ancient Greece and Rome, Mr. Long resembles Dr. Arnold?'[3] *Rugby Chapel* itself, it can now be proved, was inspired by

[1] Arnold Whitridge, *Doctor Arnold of Rugby*, Henry Holt & Co., New York, 1928, p. 214.

[2] Matthew Arnold's *Letters*, Macmillan & Co., New York, 1895, i. 362.

[3] *Essays in Criticism*, 1st series, New York, Macmillan, 1924, p. 349.

a review of *Tom Brown's Schooldays* that tried to make out the head master as a bustling religious fanatic.[1]

A little-known and highly interesting proof of Matthew Arnold's sincerity in his estimates of his father, the kind of evidence Sainte-Beuve would care about, is furnished in a letter of Stanley, written at the time of Dr. Arnold's death in 1842: 'Matthew spoke of one thing which seemed to me very natural and affecting: that the first thing which struck him when he saw the body was the thought that their sole source of *information* was gone, that all that they had ever known was contained in that lifeless head. They had consulted him so entirely on everything, and the strange feeling of their being cut off for ever one can well imagine.'[2]

Another testimony to the light in which Dr. Arnold was regarded by his pupils is that red-letter day in the life of all the Rugby men at Oxford, December 2, 1841. It was then that Arnold came up to deliver his inaugural lecture as Regius Professor of Modern History. Stanley 'saw in the commencement of Arnold's direct connexion with the University more than a tardy tribute of respect after years of obloquy and misapprehension, and more than a revival of Rugby days and a renewal of old relations of teacher and pupil. He looked forward to his lectures as the advent of a fresh invigorating breeze across a parched and sultry plain, as the counterpoise to what he considered the evil tendencies of the Oxford Movement, as the infusion of new life into the decaying professorial system. He trusted that Arnold would break down the conventional barriers which divided religious from secular learning, that he would dissipate the exclusive adoration of the Fathers and School-men among the dead, or Bishops and Pastors among the living, and that he would communicate to others the power and charm which the great writers of antiquity, the poets and philosophers of modern times, the sailors and soldiers and statesmen of the world of action, possessed as auxiliaries in the cause of religion.'[3] The audience was the largest that had ever come to hear a professor. The Rugby men

---

[1] For a new account of the origin of *Rugby Chapel*, see Appendix I.
[2] Prothero, *Letters and Verses of Arthur Penrhyn Stanley*, Scribner's, New York, 1895, p. 74.   [3] Prothero's *Stanley*, i. 306–7.

were thrilled to see Arnold at last receiving his due and producing the effect upon others that he had formerly produced upon them.

Whatever hold Dr. Arnold had upon the affections of his former pupils was eternally secured on the morning of June 11, 1842, when news of his sudden death sent a shock throughout all England. The friendship between Clough and Matthew Arnold, already in its Oxford setting, was given then a new depth and a new significance. From that day Mary Arnold and her children became the special care and devotion of a band of the finest men of England, and Clough was of that band. One sees from that time a paternal note, sincere but light enough not to be offensive, come into his every reference to Matt Arnold.

Clough heard from Stanley a full account of Dr. Arnold's death, in a hitherto unpublished letter which it seems well to present in this book.[1] It reveals as well as any other document the place to which a Rugby schoolmaster had come in the lives of his men. From that June day, as Stanley said thirty-eight years later, a circle of Rugby men were 'on a little island of memory, and all who share in that memory must hold together as long as life lasts'.[2]

If it is essential to stress the enormous hold that Matthew Arnold's father had upon Arthur Clough, it is equally important to indicate the danger that lay in that attachment. Clough was, of all men, the one who least needed one phase of Dr. Arnold's training. From his mother he had inherited and received by early teaching a high moral and religious sense. The natural sweetness and pliancy of his nature was fortunately to save him from offensiveness in these things, at least in his effect upon his friends. His abundant gusto and love of life in all its forms was too strong in him for either fanaticism or asceticism. The author of The Bothie, that poem which has perhaps as much fresh air as any poem in our language, if he knows something of Cowper's inward ways, has also Cowper's love of outward things. If he questions his own soul and the truths on which it rests, he knows Crabbe's ardent

[1] See Appendix II.
[2] A. P. Stanley to Miss Frances Arnold; letter of June 11, 1880.

6

sense for earthly fact and Chaucer's sly joy in the absurdity and loveliness of man. A born poet can never represent a system either of thought or of conscience; his very spirit will run over and escape the mould. He leaves rigidity to the philosophers and the theologians. He forgets his questions while he asks them, and loses in his zest for men and things, in the beauty and the wonder of the world, all his worry over first and final causes. The careful reader of Clough's poetry will see that he did these things, and to that degree he was a born poet. Indeed, one of the remarkable features in the letters Clough's many friends wrote to him from his youth unto his death, as their publication will some day show, is their complete *faith* in him and in his power to understand all phases of their lives. Here was the large mind and intuitive heart that could follow every strain, to which no slight detail would be unarresting, no emotion foreign. The poet's wide and luminous view they accepted in him as axiomatic. It was this that made his friends, and even those whose contact was more slight, believe him the most richly endowed man of his time, rich chiefly in the many shades and facets of his being.

On the other hand, Matthew Arnold is exactly right when he tells us in these letters that Clough was the most conscientious man he ever knew, and at times, morbidly so. One sees Arnold's continual endeavour to rouse his friend, whose radiance and genius he clearly recognized, to some unquestioning activity. There is even a fine irony in watching Dr. Arnold's son endeavour to remove from Clough an excessive habit of mind that Dr. Arnold had himself engendered, or at least fixed.

Rugby did teach boys to worry about their souls and the souls of those about them. The normal apple-eating animal doubtless profited by this suggestion. Whatever may be said against it, Rugby was sending to the universities a set of clean and fine-spirited men who, even when their priggishness had become a legend, commanded the respect and the love of those about them. But for the tender conscience Dr. Arnold's training was a doubling of itself. The letters of Clough already in print show how fagging wearied

7

him; in his unselfish but too early concern for his brother
George and in his responsibility for the lower forms of
his school, duty becomes too much a voice and too con-
stricting. What is worst of all, it made his body very tired.

During his Rugby years and the first part of his Oxford
training Clough kept journals that show clearly the in-
wardness to which he had been turned. He could not
possibly have become a prig; and these records of his
spiritual broodings, actually will, when the contents are
completely known, endear him to an understanding reader.
They explain the strange shyness by which his friends were
puzzled, as they record his constant fear that he has spoken
out too freely, his great desire being 'not to be positive in
society'. Archbishop Temple used to say that people who
had never known Clough intimately perhaps might wonder
at the extravagant notion his friends had of his genius.
And Temple said the trouble was that these casual people
had never heard Clough under way some hour past mid-
night, when, his defences down and his head overflowing
with ideas, he charmed his listeners with a magical power
peculiarly his own. But such rush and overflow of his
powerful spirits seemed to the young boy at Rugby evil
and unworthy of him. It was this *abundant* side of Clough
that Matthew Arnold came to know at Balliol; what he
probably never knew was the early effort at curbing that
very abundance, in the sense that the too fast and brilliant
working of one's mind was somehow wrong and alien to
some deeper quiet of the heart. 'Have been a good deal
excited—intellectually—little spiritually—living much too
fast', he records on an August evening of 1835, when he
was but sixteen years old.[1]

A fortnight later he reflects, 'O the night is very dark—
but what must it be in Hell, where darkness is as light, as
universal, as all pervading'. And this, of Sunday morning,
in September: 'Instead of turning to God last night I wrote
a sonnet, and poetized till 10 o'clock. Composed 2 more
in bed.'

Such is not the training of poets. They should not
pass their schooldays in worrying over young hoodlums

[1] Clough MSS. (journals).

8

who have not their fineness of perception; nor should even their love of Dr. Arnold disturb them too much about the condition of the lower forms. This anti-poetic influence of Rugby has probably impressed some writers [1] unduly; but we should not ignore it altogether. And Mr. Osborne is probably near the truth when he suggests that Clough, busying his body and his soul in the rigours of going to school, had not sufficient time for that 'wish-thinking' which is the making of the creative artist. Young Marlowe amid the jewelled pageantry of Canterbury, Shelley seeking his ghosts within a starlit wood, and Tennyson listening to the mystical cadences of his own name are without question nearer to the muse that fires the passion and the sensuousness of verse.

Nevertheless all this is too easy to overdo. Whatever one finds in these anxious early letters and journals, one must not forget that Arthur Clough was authentically a poet and a critic. Had he not been, he could hardly have had the effect he did on Matthew Arnold. And both by his poetic nature and by his critical insight, he was protected against the excess of Rugby. That he sensed his peril clearly is shown in some of the letters he wrote while there. In his epilogue to the later *Dipsychus*, moreover, he gives us, not only his estimate of Rugby and Dr. Arnold, but also the living proof that Rugby did not hurt him deeply. The average reader, to whom Clough has become only the sad image of Victorian unrest, does well to know this lively critique. It proves by its own zest and cleverness that the Rugby it satirizes did not crush small boys so permanently as it is often supposed to have done. The Matthew Arnold of *Friendship's Garland* must have enjoyed it hugely. The poet is represented as addressing his uncle:

' "You see, dear sir, the thing which it is attempted to represent is the conflict between the tender conscience and the world...."

' "Oh, for goodness' sake, my dear boy," interrupted my uncle, "don't go into the theory of it. If you're wrong in it, it makes bad worse; if you're right, you may be a critic, but you can't be a poet. . . . But as for that, I quite agree that

[1] For a well-written and brilliant example see James I. Osborne, *Arthur Hugh Clough*, London, 1920, pp. 26–8.

9

consciences are much too tender in your generation—schoolboys' consciences, too! As my old friend the Canon says of
the Westminster students, 'They're all so pious.' It's all
Arnold's doing; he spoilt the public schools."

'"My dear uncle," said I, "how can so venerable a sexa-
genarian utter so juvenile a paradox? How often have I not
heard you lament the idleness and listlessness, the boorishness
and vulgar tyranny, the brutish manners alike, and minds——"

'"Ah!" said my uncle, "I may have fallen in occasionally
with the talk of the day; but at seventy one begins to see clearer
into the bottom of one's mind. . . . 'Young men must be young
men,' as the worthy head of your college said to me touching a
case of rustication. 'My dear sir,' said I, 'I only wish to heaven
they would be; but as for my own nephews, they seem to me
a sort of hobbadi-hoy cherub, too big to be innocent, and too
simple for anything else. They're full of the notion of the world
being so wicked and of their taking a higher line, as they call
it. I only fear they'll never take any line at all.' What is the
true purpose of education? Simply to make plain to the young
understanding the laws of the life they will have to enter.
For example—that lying won't do, thieving still less; that
idleness will get punished; that if they are cowards, the whole
world will be against them; that if they will have their own
way, they must fight for it. As for the conscience, mamma,
I take it has probably set that agoing fast enough already.
What a blessing to see her good little child come back a brave
young devil-may-care!"

'"Exactly, my dear sir. As if at twelve or fourteen a round-
about boy, with his three meals a day inside him, is likely to
be over-troubled with scruples."

'"Put him through a strong course of confirmation and
sacraments, backed up with sermons and private admonitions,
and what is much the same as auricular confession, and really,
my dear nephew, I can't answer for it but he mayn't turn out
as great a goose as you—pardon me—*were* about the age of
eighteen or nineteen."

'" . . . You see, my dear sir, you must not refer it to Arnold,
at all at all. Anything that Arnold did in this direction . . ."

'"Why, my dear boy, how often have I not heard from you,
how he used to attack offences, not as offences—the right view
—against discipline, but as sin, heinous guilt, I don't know
what beside! Why didn't he flog them and hold his tongue?
Flog them he did, but why preach?"

'"If he did err in this way, sir, which I hardly think, I

ascribe it to the spirit of the time. The real cause of the evil you complain of, which to a certain extent I admit, was, I take it, the religious movement of the last century, beginning with Wesleyanism, and culminating at last in Puseyism. This over-excitation of the religious sense, resulting in this irrational, almost animal irritability of conscience, was, in many ways, as foreign to Arnold as it is proper to . . ."

' "Well, well, my dear nephew, if you like to make a theory of it, pray write it out for yourself nicely in full; but your poor old uncle does not like theories, and is moreover sadly sleepy!" ' [1]

Just where one is to bear down and where one is to go lightly here is not too plain. But the man who could write such a passage was not long to be taken in by anything. Then, too, if Clough was defended against Rugby by his poetical nature and by his critical insight, he had also more ordinary escape. He owned the best of good tempers. His fellows generally liked him, even those who were greatly different from him. Dean Bradley recalled that when he entered Rugby, a few days after Clough had left it for Oxford, the lad who later became the famous Major Hodson, of 'Hodson's Horse', said to him, 'What a fool you were not to come a week earlier—because then you could have said one day that you had been at school with Tom Clough!' [2] He was the friend and adviser of his fellows in small matters as well as great ones, and he was a leader in their games. So well, moreover, did he do his lessons, that Dr. Arnold, who never commented in delivering prizes, broke his rule to congratulate him publicly on having won every possible honour that Rugby had to give.

Perhaps Clough's real passion at school, and his way of trying to show his appreciation of Dr. Arnold, was his care for the *Rugby Magazine*. This periodical, founded after the example of Eton, was, so its youthful managers thought, going to set Rugby before the world.[3] Clough's correspondence with men who had gone on to Oxford and Cambridge is filled with concern for it and with entreaties

[1] A. H. C.'s *Poems*, London, 1913, pp. 167–70.
[2] From a manuscript memoir of Clough by G. G. Bradley.
[3] The first issue appeared in July 1835. Eight numbers followed, almost quarterly, until November 1837.

for contributions. There is in the back of one of his Rugby journals a formal prayer for the new venture. It is worth complete quotation, because it shows very well the attractive blend of earnestness and sweetness that was the key to his character. It is, on first reading, a prayer that one might expect from a typical Rugby schoolboy; to discerning eyes, however, it will hold something more:

About the Magazine

O all-wise God, whose Providence has ordained this undertaking, and laid its weight on me, grant that it be not a snare unto me. Let it not interfere with those more especial duties which I am placed here to perform,—with my efforts to improve myself in knowledge and intellectual power so as to be better fit for the duties of my future life,—far less with those I should ever be making for my own spiritual improvement, and that of my companions. Spacious Father, give me thy Holy Spirit whilst I am busied in this work, that neither by the sense of intellectual power or the praises of others my foolish and wicked vanity be excited in me. But let thy purifying influence so continually dwell in me, that this work may be indeed done unto the Lord, that I may seek in it not the selfish gratification of my own desires, but the increase of reputation to this *my* school, and, in some degrèe also, thine, and the spread of those higher principles whose light shines here through all of the same age everywhere. Grant also, Lord, that these its objects may be fulfilled to the utmost, and that it may be an instrument in thy hands of great good to this School and all boys everywhere. And these things I pray for, O Lord, in his name who hath told us to ask, for we shall receive, our Lord Jesus Christ.

These are Rugby sentiments and feelings, and the serious concern frightens one a little. But the young voice that speaks here will never be the voice of a prig.

Clough crowned his Rugby days by winning the Balliol Scholarship in November 1836, to the intense delight of Dr. Arnold. The following October he began, at the age of eighteen, an Oxford career that was to last, first at Balliol and then at Oriel, for eleven years, or over one-fourth of his entire life. He went with the full conviction of those at Rugby that he was destined for great things. Even the

Oxford dons who bent to his examination grew warm with excitement at the reading of his youthful English essay. The Rugby men already at Oxford welcomed him as a justification of their school. Dr. Arnold wrote the following hitherto unpublished letter to the Rev. A. B. Clough, Arthur's uncle at Jesus College:

Rugby, October 19, 1837.

My dear Sir,

I did not write to you when your nephew left us, but I must take the opportunity of one of our Men's going to Oxford tomorrow, to send you these few Lines. . . . I cannot resist my Desire of congratulating you most heartily on the delightful Close of your Nephew's long Career at Rugby;—where he has passed eight years without a Fault, so far as the School is concerned, where he has gone on ripening gradually in all Excellence intellectual and spiritual,—and from whence he has now gone to Oxford, not only full of Honours,—but carrying with him the Respect and Love of all whom he has left behind,—and regarded by myself, I may truly say, with an Affection and Interest hardly less than I should feel for my own Son.—I only hope,—and indeed nothing doubt,—that you will have the same Pleasure in watching his Career in Oxford, that I have long had in watching it at Rugby.—

Our Speeches have been transferred from Easter to the third week in June, which I hope will suit our Oxford Friends as well.—And although your personal Connection with Rugby is at an End, yet I hope that we shall have the Pleasure of seeing you here from Time to Time amongst us, as we had before your Nephew left us.—

Believe me to be
My dear Sir,
Very truly your's,
T. Arnold.

Matthew Arnold was almost fifteen years old when his father wrote that letter. Not until four years later was he to join Clough in Oxford, and in that four years many changes were to take place. When Arthur Clough entered Balliol, Oxford was in the full stir of the Tractarian Movement. Its effect upon him, at least any full analysis of his attitude towards the theological principles involved, is hardly our concern. He went up fearing what lay before him, because

13

Newmanism had long drawn the full, and certainly not always just, fire of Dr. Arnold.[1] Yet he could not have missed the influence of Newman had he desired to do so; for Newman, like Dr. Arnold, told upon men more even by what he was than by what he taught. There is a significant entry in Clough's manuscript diary for Monday of Passion Week, 1838: 'I must keep in mind . . . that many persons of the most advanced piety and goodness are this week engaged in all sorts of self-denial, and mortification—fasting from food and sleep, amusement and society—Newman for instance, whose errors as we believe them to be must not make me ever forget how far he is above me in goodness and piety, and wisdom too—tho' in certain points we with less power may by our advantages be nearer the real truth, and though less wise have more wisdom.'

Matthew Arnold later saw in Newman a wonderful exhibition of English style and un-English urbanity,[2] and in the Oxford Movement itself, not so much a religious deliverance, as a protest of 'beauty and sweetness' against middle-class liberalism and middle-class Protestantism with its hardness, and hideousness, and grotesque illusions.[3] For his American audiences in 1883 he recalls the voices of the early Oxford days, and Newman's with that of Carlyle

[1] On May 24, 1836, he had written to Stanley: 'Now with regard to the Newmanites. I do not call them bad men, nor would I deny their many good qualities. . . . I judge of them as I do commonly of mixed characters, where the noble and the base, the good and the bad, are strangely mixed up together . . . but fanaticism is idolatry, and it has the moral evil of idolatry in it—that is, a fanatic worships something which is the creature of his own devices, and thus even his self-devotion in support of it is only an apparent self-sacrifice, for it is in fact making the parts of his nature or his mind which he least values, offer sacrifice to that which he most values. The moral fault, as it appears to me, is in the idolatry—the setting up some idea which is most kindred to our own minds, and then putting it in the place of Christ, who alone cannot be made an idol, and cannot inspire fanaticism, because He combines all ideas of perfection, and exhibits them in their just harmony and combination.' A. P. Stanley, *The Life and Correspondence of Thomas Arnold, D.D.*, London, 1892, ii. 35–6.

[2] See Mrs. Humphry Ward, *A Writer's Recollections*, Collins, London, 1919, pp. 11–12. And Arnold's *Literary Influence of Academies*, Essays in Criticism, 1st series, Macmillan, New York, 1924, pp. 60–1.

[3] *Culture and Anarchy*, Macmillan, New York, 1924, pp. 28–30.

and Emerson: 'Who could resist the charm of that spiritual apparition, gliding in the dim afternoon light through the aisles of St. Mary's, rising into the pulpit, and then, in the most entrancing of voices, breaking the silence with words and thoughts which were a religious music,—subtle, sweet, mournful? I seem to hear him still, saying: "After the fever of life, after wearinesses and sicknesses, fightings and despondings, languor and fretfulness, struggling and succeeding; after all the changes and chances of this troubled, unhealthy state—at length comes death, at length the white throne of God, at length the beatific vision." '[1]

Newmanism certainly went farther with Clough than that. He examined closely the doctrinal points of the Tracts. In his letters he frequently retails the progress of these doctrines,[2] discovering in time that certain oppositions to Evangelical and Calvinistic Christianity strongly appeal to him. As early as the spring of 1838, he confesses that he likes Newman much better than he did and admires him exceedingly in many points; moreover, that he counts Hurrell Froude's *Remains* among the most instructive books he has ever read.[3] But Tractarianism could not attach him to any new position. What it really did was to set up at Oxford an atmosphere of extreme religious speculation and excitement that left him quite unsettled and absorbed more of his valuable time and energy and poetic dreaming than the Rugby duties had ever done. As his friend Gell in April 1843 wrote to him from Van Diemen's Land, 'You seem to be in the midst of the Oxford heresies without having suffered much beyond a good puzzling.'[4]

This very puzzling, however, was the mischief. It would be hard to conceive a change more abrupt than that of coming from Dr. Arnold to live at Balliol in 1837. At Rugby one had served God by getting one's lessons and maintaining a certain purity of mind. But in the all-consuming days of the Tracts any routine of study seemed tame business. At that time, at least, Oxford could not be loved because 'the

[1] *Discourses in America*, Macmillan, New York, 1924, pp. 139–40.
[2] See his letters to J. P. Gell, *Prose Remains*, pp. 78–81.
[3] *Prose Remains*, p. 77, and Clough MSS.   [4] Clough MSS.

world was in her heart'. The humanities took minor place. The city was a narrow one of puzzled heads and wagging tongues; and young men of promise, who should have been pegging away at mathematics and their Greek and Latin verses, gave themselves over entirely to discussions of fore-knowledge, will, and fate. 'If it had not been for the Class List,' Goldwin Smith tells us, 'which kept a certain number of us working at classics and mathematics, the University would have become a mere battlefield of theologians.' [1]

The most important man in Clough's early days at Balliol was William George Ward, who from Tractarianism later followed Newman to Rome. Officially he was Clough's tutor in mathematics. Actually he was a kind of speculative logic-machine whose supreme delight was to make proselytes by starting a destructive line of thought, to be replaced, if the experiment turned out happily, by constructive notions. He was, as Jowett, whom he initiated into metaphysics, said of him, 'a kind of Silenus-Socrates, whose delight it was to deliver young men of their doubts'.[2] There are many pictures of him in the reminiscences of Oxford men. Goldwin Smith remembers his almost Falstaffian figure; 'though very fat, he walked with a sort of skip, and wore low loose shoes which he had a trick of kicking off. . . . There was something laughable about all that he said or did.'[3] Stanley admired his honesty, his fearless love of truth, and his argufying power; but he sensed Ward's one-sided development of a gigantic logical faculty at the expense of the rest of his nature.[4]

Very early Ward sought out Clough, partly because he honoured any one who had been a disciple of Dr. Arnold, and partly because he recognized in the new Balliol scholar a congenial power of thought and a desire for truth. So he began to turn his young pupil's mind inside out. The

[1] *Goldwin Smith's Correspondence*, edited by Arnold Haultain, Laurie, London [1913?], p. 269.
[2] Abbott and Campbell, *Life and Letters of Benjamin Jowett*, London, 1897, i. 73–4.
[3] Goldwin Smith's *Reminiscences*, edited by Arnold Haultain, Macmillan, New York, 1910, pp. 63–4.
[4] Prothero, *Stanley*, i. 168–9.

Oxford curriculum did not offer Clough enough to keep him busy.[1] He had time in abundance on his hands for all kinds of questionings. 'If you were to come here', he writes to Gell, 'you would at once have Ward at you asking you your opinions on every possible subject . . . beginning with Covent Garden and Macready and certainly not ending till you got to the Question of the Moral Sense and Deontology. I do not quite like hearing so much of these Matters as I do—but I suppose if one can only keep steadily to one's work (which I wish I did) and quite resolve to forget all the words one has heard and to theorize only for amusement, there is no harm in it.'[2]

Clough's daily entries in his journals show, however, that he became even more sensitive to the harm in these gyrations, although enjoying Ward and being fascinated by his stimulating company. His own basic religious feeling, rooted in him by nature and training, seemed alien to the logical designs that were fashioning and changing in his head. He who had passionately worked for Rugby was now left to idle wanderings. The trouble was that Clough was so sincere and downright about his thinking, that he could not play with ideas and marshal hypotheses for his own amusement. Truth was precious and immediate to him, or else, of necessity, far away. In October 1839 he writes: 'I only hope to escape the vortex of Philosophism and Discussion (whereof Ward is the Centre), as it is the most exhausting exercise in the world: and I assure you I quite makarize you at Cambridge for your liberty from it. It seems to have a different effect on Stanley and Lake, but I do not think it can be wholly beneficial to anyone. The Contrast of home is great.'[3]

Ward genuinely loved Clough, and no one has left him fairer tribute. Few have seen more clearly at once Clough's power and singular unworldliness and sweetness of disposition. Next to Newman, he seemed to his tutor the most attractive person at Oxford. And Ward's own

[1] See some interesting autobiographical matter in his review of the Oxford University Commissioners' Report in *Prose Remains*, pp. 399 ff.
[2] A. H. C., *Prose Remains*, p. 80 (text corrected by original MS.).
[3] *Prose Remains*, p. 85, with additions from the original MS. letter.

account of their friendship, apart from the important information it gives, is a rare document in the history of human candours:

'What was before all things to have been desired for him was that, during his undergraduate course, he should have given himself up thoroughly to his classical and mathematical studies; that he should have kept up . . . the habits of prayer and Scripture-reading which he brought with him from Rugby, but should have kept himself aloof from plunging prematurely into the theological controversies then so rife at Oxford. He would thus indeed have unconsciously grown clear of a certain narrowness of sympathy with which he naturally commenced his Oxford life, and would have acquired a general knowledge of what those points were which at that time were so keenly debated around him; but at the same time he would have been saved from all injury to the gradual and healthy growth of his mind and character. . . . I fear that, from my point of view, I must account it the great calamity of his life that he was brought into contact with myself. My whole interest at that time (as now) was concentrated on questions which to me seem the most important and interesting that can occupy the mind. Nor was there any reason why they should not occupy my mind, considering my age and position. It was a very different thing to force them prematurely on the attention of a young man just coming up to college, and to drive him, as it were, peremptorily into a decision upon them; to aim at making him as hot a partisan as I was myself. My own influence by itself might not have done much, but it was powerfully seconded by the general spirit of Oxford society at that time, and by the power which Mr. Newman then wielded throughout the University.

'The result was not surprising. I had been prematurely forcing Clough's mind, and there came a reaction. His intellectual perplexity for some time preyed heavily upon his spirits; it grievously interfered with his studies; and I take for granted it must have very seriously disturbed his religious practices and habits. I cannot to this day think of all this without a bitter pang of self-reproach.' [1]

The immediate practical effect of Clough's Oxford experience was his lowered academic performance. He

[1] Wilfrid Ward, *William George Ward and the Oxford Movement*, Macmillan, London and New York, 1889, pp. 109–10.

18

had been satiated with prizes at Rugby; and his private journals, even more than do his letters, show how his real problem at Oxford was, not the work of the schools, but a mastering of himself in a time when he felt his solid ground somewhat slipping away from beneath his feet. These same journals show that, as far as winning special honours, he was moved only by a desire to help his father's financial burden and to please Dr. Arnold. But he took only a second class. Tom Arnold gives us a picture of the reports that came back to Rugby. 'We heard', he says, 'that he did not carry all before him, as we thought he ought to have done; and without in the least altering our opinion of his intellectual strength, we speculated on what could be the cause of failure. I remember—it must have been, I think, after his comparative failure in the schools in 1841—his coming up to my father in the front court of the School-house, standing in front of him with face partly flushed and partly pale, and simply saying, "I have failed." My father looked gravely and kindly at him, but what he said in reply I do not remember, or whether he said anything.' [1] This missing a first class was the cause of a mild sensation. Clough was the first Balliol scholar to go below the mark since the beginning of the lists; and when Oxford men heard the news they could not believe their ears. Their entire faith in the whole system of academic awards was materially weakened.

Clough then tried for the Balliol fellowship in the autumn of 1841, and was again unsuccessful. Arthur Stanley gave in a letter the feeling of the Rugby friends: 'Perhaps you do not need consolation. But to me, partly for his sake, partly for the sake of Balliol, it seemed so great a misfortune that I cannot help venting my lamentations over it. But there is this great comfort. Some of his papers were done so splendidly as fully to show that the spring of genius has not yet been dried up within him, and therefore I hope he will get in at Oriel. Not that I ever thought that the genius was gone; but I feared that the power of expressing it to the world was gone. What a singular person he is! I, of course, never having been intimate with him,

[1] *The Nineteenth Century*, xliii (1898), p. 106.

can only reverence him at a respectful distance. But the little I do know of him has always made me think and maintain that he is the profoundest man of his years that I ever saw, or that Rugby ever sent forth. His very misfortunes invest him with a kind of sacredness, for, academically speaking, who ever was so unfortunate—so able, so laborious, and yet so unaccountably failing?'[1]

On the Friday morning of Easter week, 1842, however, Clough was elected a fellow of Oriel, where Dr. Arnold had been before him and where Matthew Arnold was to come later. Newman assisted at the examination, the last in which he ever took part. Thus Dr. Arnold shortly before his death was allowed once more to enjoy the success of his protégé.

Matthew Arnold, meantime, had won on his own account the Balliol scholarship. On November 10, 1841, Clough notifies his friend Gell, out in Van Diemen's Land: 'Mat. Arnold has come up to reside as scholar of Balliol, and as a report whispered to me (which as you are a long way off I will venture to send you) has been going out with the Harriers.'[2]

Tom Arnold came up the following year. The two brothers, together with Clough and Theodore Walrond, proceed to form 'a little interior company'. They go skiffing up the Cherwell and in the little network of streams that lace the meadows by Iffley and Sandford. Finally it is arranged that the four shall breakfast each Sunday morning in Clough's rooms. There they talk of Sir Robert Peel, Carlyle, and Emerson; they grow heated about the Irish problem; and hold long discussions over the leading articles in the *Spectator*.[3] George Sand seems, in her novels, the incarnation of a new spirit of revolt and renovation; and in addition, there is the subtle pleasure of feeling just a trifle wicked in reading her.[4] The Decade, a small society that meets in the members' rooms to debate all things past and new, takes also a large share of their time.[5] Gradually in

[1] Prothero, *Letters and Verses of Stanley*, p. 65.   [2] Clough MSS.
[3] *The Nineteenth Century*, xliii (1898), 106–7.
[4] Mrs. Ward, *A Writer's Recollections*, p. 12.
[5] John Duke Coleridge, Benjamin Jowett, J. C. Shairp, W. C.

the evening discussions of this little group Clough begins to reveal the power that his contemporaries were to remember for the rest of their lives.

It is one of the ironies of English literature that the friendship formed in these Oxford days between Arnold and Clough has been immortalized in a poem which probably does not suggest its chief ground. When he wrote *Thyrsis*, Arnold well knew he was selecting one aspect of Clough, the ideal side; so strongly did he feel this that he did not even send the poem to Mrs. Clough. This side was a true one, indeed, the memory of which, in his middle years, probably sustained a busy inspector of schools, trying to keep alive amid the 'great town's harsh, heart-wearying roar'. It was Clough's single-minded love of Truth, his conviction that some spark from Heaven *ought* to fall and was worth waiting for, that struck all his friends and made Carlyle and Emerson his advocates. But, even so, *Thyrsis* has put a label upon Clough. All some very cultured people know of him to-day is that 'his piping took a troubled sound'. It is no conceit to realize that, if Arnold's poem has fixed one aspect of his friend and given him an extra fame, it has helped to obscure and prevent the knowledge of that other Clough, high-spirited, deeply imaginative, and full of gusto. It has let critics rest content to see in *Dipsychus* a conventional lament for faith

Lake, James Riddell, Arthur Stanley, R. W. Church, and Frederick Temple were among the Decade's distinguished members. Mrs. Clough has left some very full notes of a conversation she had with Temple on February 8, 1862: 'Dr. Temple spoke of his [Arthur Clough's] power of speaking, of his appearing in a debating Society called the Decade—especially of one speech on the future politics of the world, the connexion of the world and of the Church. He said the grandeur of the thought and the splendour of the language quite carried him away. . . . He said that he had great influence, that those immediately succeeding him (next to his contemporaries) felt they owed more to him than to any other man, that he himself had seen a great deal of him owing to their habit of dining together at the same table; that he disliked influencing men. Once Dr. Temple had expressed some opinion, when A. said, "Why, you thought differently six months ago." Dr. Temple said, "Yes, but you knocked that out of me." He remembered the kind of shrinking when A. heard that.' (See also J. C. Shairp's recollection of Clough at the Decade, in *Prose Remains*, pp. 26–7.)

departed, rather than a humorous and penetrating psychological study. Clough has paid his toll, of course, for the real defects that mar his verse, and for these Matthew Arnold is not responsible. These letters reveal clearly how he tries to point Clough to poetical advance. But by putting in light one aspect of *Thyrsis*, he has helped blind us to others. We have forgotten that Corydon once *had* a rival, and a very good one!

It is Tom Arnold who gives us more of the truth. He too recognized Clough's ideal side. But he blends it with other qualities. Out in New Zealand he remembers the Oxford days and writes: 'How little do I know of all that capacious head of yours is scheming and imagining.'[1] And again: 'I have often thought of your jolly old countenance, and longed for a sight of it; especially when walking alone in the forests or among the hills of this beautiful country.'

It was this jolly countenance and the capacious, scheming head that Matt Arnold relished in the Oriel fellow, as much as any 'fugitive or gracious light' he sought. For Clough, with all his shy ways, had abundant charm, especially when he let himself go. 'I can talk tremendous!' he confessed one day, for once not ashamed of this achievement. It was this talkative, buoyant Clough, one can hardly help feeling, that first drew Arnold so strongly to him.

Certainly the two friends had much in common. They were both fond of poetry and the practice of it. Clough was at work on those things that later made up the *Ambarvalia*, and Arnold was preparing his own first volume. They both had a liking for classical literature and for the new world that was opening on the Continent. And *Thyrsis* does consecrate, at least, their mutual love of the countryside round Oxford, a scene that Dr. Arnold had enjoyed before them. They shared, moreover, a strong social passion that, if it were more pronounced at first in Clough, who wrote upon the Irish famine and confessed Republican views, had its place also in Dr. Arnold's son, as the letters in this volume clearly show.

It must be remembered, too, that his duties at Oriel and

[1] MS. letters of Thomas Arnold to A. H. C. of September 14, 1851, and of June 26, 1848, respectively.

his gradual weariness of theological reflection had restored Clough's poise, even in profound spiritual matters. During the time Matthew Arnold knew him at Oxford he was falling back upon his own morality and character, wherein the intuitions of his faith lay, and thinking less about positive proofs and the importance of them. In fact, Arnold was going through the same process, endeavouring to find some new statement of a faith that had ceased to repose upon dogma and creed. Both were hunting for 'higher, holier things than these'.

Clough's actual problem came to be, of course, the question of his own honesty in continuing in a university where one was obliged to subscribe to the Thirty-nine Articles of the Church of England. 'It is not so much from any definite objection to this or that point, as general dislike to subscription, and strong feeling of its being a bondage and a very heavy one, and one that may cramp and cripple one for life.'[1] Some nine months later he informs Gell[2] that he has signed the Articles, although he is not sure he has been justified in doing so. 'However, I have for the present laid by that perplexity, though it may perhaps recur some time or other. . . .' Recur it did, and eventually led to Clough's resigning his fellowship in 1848, when 'Thyrsis of his own will went away'.

If Arthur Clough grew impatient of the Thirty-nine Articles, he found agreement in his friend. After Arnold's death in 1888, Edward Walford, a former scholar of Balliol, wrote an interesting letter to *The Times*, which contained the following: 'I am the only survivor of a batch of five freshmen who were matriculated at Balliol on Nov. 28, 1840; and I well remember how, when we waited in the Vice-Chancellor's ante-room for admission, Arnold

---

[1] *Prose Remains*, p. 91.

[2] Gell's letters from Van Diemen's Land were among the most steadying influences Clough received during his university days. On May 31, 1844, Gell wrote from Hobart Town: 'Nothing would surprise me after your last letter, not even to learn that you were turned into an Independent Clergyman. Pray why not sign the XXXIX articles; you must sign something, unless you mean to have nothing to do with anybody. Where will you find a more sensible set of clerical regulations?' (Clough MSS.)

23

professed to us his great aversion to sundry statements in the Thirty-nine Articles, which at that time we were all forced to subscribe, especially that article which expresses an approval of the Athanasian Creed, and that which denounces and renounces the Pope of Rome. In his early days, when we dined at the same scholars' table, I shall never forget how, in opposition to the Tractarianism of the day, he used to say that the strict imposition of creeds had done more to break up than to unite churches, and nations, and families, and how even then, in our small and highly privileged circle, he was the apostle of religious toleration in every direction. His cheerfulness, geniality, and universal charity combined to make him as general a favourite at Balliol as he became afterwards in the wider world of society in London.' [1]

For those who could understand him and the contradictions that he offered, the Matt Arnold of the Balliol and Oriel days must have been as fascinating as he was provoking. There is hardly a question that, despite his reverence for his father, he was determined, in some respects, not to be Dr. Arnold's son. He gave himself many airs, affected French ways, dressed rather grandly, and indulged a general bumptiousness as good-natured as it was superficial. Almost every reference to him, both in the Clough correspondence and elsewhere, shows that his friends hardly knew what he would do next to astonish them. All this is very refreshing to discover in one who, in spite of his continual humour, has conventionally represented the grand style and the proprieties of culture. One of the charming aspects of his letters to Clough is the very extravagance and absurdity of some of them, especially the early ones. A few of them are quite mad. It is consoling to know that not always, at any rate, was Arnold possessed of 'balance, lucidity, proportion', and the other graces he later so entirely made his own.

At Oxford he was rather a social lion, his keen, bantering talk continuing, even after Goethe had begun to replace Byron in his affection.[2] Max Müller saw the charm of

---

[1] Edition of Friday, April 20, 1888, p. 13.
[2] Thomas Arnold, *Passages in a Wandering Life*, pp. 56–7.

Arnold as an undergraduate and recalled 'he was beautiful as a young man, strong and manly, full of dreams and schemes. His Olympian manners began even at Oxford; there was no harm in them. . . . The sound of his voice and the wave of his arm were Jove-like.'[1] Clough himself gives some striking evidence in a previously unpublished letter to Shairp, doubtless of the Oriel period: 'Matt is full of Parisianism; Theatres in general, and Rachel in special: he enters the room with a chanson of Beranger's on his lips—for the sake of French words almost conscious of tune:[2] his carriage shows him in fancy parading the Rue de Rivoli; and his hair is guiltless of English scissors: he breakfasts at 12, and never dines in Hall, and in the week or 8 days rather (for 2 Sundays must be included) he has been to Chapel *once*.'

Arnold's light, debonair ways were not always understood or appreciated by his friends. In his twenty-first year he wrote to his friend John Duke Coleridge: 'It is difficult for me to know in what terms to express myself after your last letter, so completely is it penetrated with that unfortunate error as to my want of interest in my friends which you say they have begun to attribute to me. It is an old subject which I need not discuss over again with you. The accusation, as you say, is not true. I laugh too much and they make one's laughter mean too much. However, the result is that when one wishes to be serious one cannot but fear a half suspicion on one's friends' parts that one is laughing, and, so, the difficulty gets worse and worse.'[3]

The difficulty did not cease with the Oxford years. 'I

[1] Laurence Hutton, *Literary Landmarks of Oxford*, Scribner's, New York, 1903, p. 43.

[2] This is a further evidence of Arnold's lack of an ear for music, a point on which he himself is quite frank. He writes to his sister of Norwich cathedral, where 'the music was so good as powerfully to impress even me' (*Letters*, i. 163). And Professor Karl Young delights to point out Arnold's confession from Munich that he has been at the opera to '*see*' (of all pieces!) Wagner's '*Tristram and Iseult*' (*Letters*, ii. 374). One is quite prepared by that for the announcement, a fortnight later, that Wagner's poetic libretto fascinates him, though 'the music says little' (*Letters*, ii. 378).

[3] E. H. Coleridge, *The Life and Correspondence of John Duke Coleridge*, Appleton, New York, 1904, i. 145–6.

think it was somewhere about 1880', writes Mrs. Sellar, 'that we met Mr. Matthew Arnold at dinner at the Sandars' in London. I had met him once before at Balliol, so had, in a way, got accustomed to the "grand manner" which was characteristic of him, and which—though it savoured of affectation—was really natural to him, and, unlike most seeming affectations, was neither repellent nor did it put you off your ease. I could not help, though, thinking of the effect it produced on that earnest-minded, somewhat prim, shy little genius, Miss Brontë, who thus writes of him: "Striking and prepossessing in appearance, his manner displeases from its seeming foppery. I own it caused me at first to regard him with regretful surprise: the shade of Dr Arnold seemed to me to frown on his young representative. Ere long a real modesty appeared under his assumed conceit, and genuine intellectual aspirations, as well as high educational acquirements, displaced superficial affectations." [1] This seems rather breaking the butterfly of a mannerism on an iron wheel of Johnsonian criticism! He was quite aware of the effect his manner had on many, and was often very humorous about it, as when he said to an old Oxford friend shortly after his marriage, "You'll like my Lucy; she has all my sweetness and none of my airs!" [2]

It is no secret that when Arnold's first volume of poems appeared in 1849 his own family was startled at the profundity and serious depth they revealed. His sister wrote at the time: 'It is the moral strength, or, at any rate, the *moral consciousness* which struck and surprised me so much in the poems. I could have been prepared for any degree of poetical power, for there being a great deal more than I

[1] Crabb Robinson wrote to his brother on May 24, 1850: 'I had an agreeable breakf^t at home on Sunday last . . . I had with me Matth. Arnold the Son of the eminent D.D. and Schoolmaster . . . a poet and private Secretary to Lord Lansdown, a very gentlemanly young man, with a light tinge of the fop that does no harm when blended with talents, good nature and high spirits. . . .' Clough was also there that morning. (*The Correspondence of Henry Crabb Robinson with the Wordsworth Circle*, edited by Edith J. Morley, Oxford, 1927, ii. 743.)

[2] E. M. Sellar, *Recollections and Impressions*, Blackwood, Edinburgh and London, 1907, pp. 151–2.

could at all appreciate; but there is something altogether different from this, something which such a man as Clough has, for instance, which I did not expect to find in Matt; but it is there.'[1]

The key to Arnold's dual nature, it seems to me, he has given us fairly well in his sonnet, *The Austerity of Poetry*. It tells, one will remember, of the young bride of Giacopone di Todi, who was killed in the fall of a platform at a public feast. When her shining outer raiment was drawn off, there was a robe of sackcloth next the smooth, white skin:

> Such, poets, is your bride, the Muse! young, gay,
> Radiant, adorn'd outside; a hidden ground
> Of thought and of austerity within.

Or, again, in his note-books, he writes for June 20, 1867: 'Not to sleep after dinner'; whereupon, a few days later, he remembers 'la gaieté—qui lui était commune avec toutes les belles âmes'.[2] Hebraism and Hellenism it is—clear enough to the later readers of *Culture and Anarchy*, but somewhat perplexing to those who knew him only as the amazing young man of Balliol.

How much Arthur Clough had to do with deepening his younger friend is hard to say. The depth was, to be sure, already there; it only needed sounding. And in this last work Clough unquestionably had a part. Arnold himself reveals in this correspondence that no other person's influence upon his life was quite so strong and so affecting This history of souls is too subtle to write of confidently, and I have no zeal for such work here. Any reader of the letters will be quite within his rights, however, in allowing a play of fancy over the text.

It is at least certain that Clough grew deeply concerned over some of Arnold's practical difficulties. The time for paper work at Balliol was coming on, and there was grave danger for an unprepared young man. On March 11, 1843, J. Manley Hawker had written to John Duke Coleridge, 'Our friend Matt utters as many absurdities as ever,

[1] *A Writer's Recollections*, p. 45.
[2] From Matthew Arnold's manuscript note-books, soon to be published in full.

with as grave a face,[1] and I am afraid wastes his time considerably, which I deeply regret, but advice does not go for much with him, and perhaps I am not well qualified to give it.'[2] When it finally seemed that Arnold might go below even a second class at Balliol, Clough took a hand. In July 1844, the two of them went into the north for what should have been a reading period. A hitherto unpublished letter from Clough to his fellow-poet Burbidge gives the scene very well. It is Sunday, July 21: 'For this evening, Mat is away; a party of Oxford visitants from Ambleside and Grasmere came over last night to spend the weekly holiday; hospitalities were required, slowdoms to be borne with: so Mat improvised a necessity to visit his Penates, and left the *onus entertainendi* upon me, departing after Morning Services. . . . I left Liverpool last Monday; slept at Fox How. Mrs. Arnold was well and kind, but somewhat anxious about Mat . . . Mat has done something this week, but this foolish walk today will lose him all tomorrow I have no doubt. . . . To tell you the sincerest truth, my dear, I am anything but sorry, but rather exceedingly glad . . . to have Mat away this blessed Monday morning. I have had but little holiday as yet myself, having been as thou well knowest, busily employed for a whole extra fortnight at Oxford in writing Biographies and Sonnets, and when Mat is here, I am painfully coerced to my work by the assurance that should I relax in the least my yokefellow would at once come to a dead stop. . . . To what extent of truancy thinkest thou may I go without chances of detection or loss of my Mentorial character? Yet have I

[1] It is from Hawker that we get one of the most entertaining pictures of Arnold's youth. He writes from Devonshire, July 3, 1843: 'We arrived here on Friday evening after sundry displays of the most consummate coolness on the part of our friend Matt, who pleasantly induced a belief into the passengers of the coach that I was a poor mad gentleman, and that he was my keeper. . . . This is a stupid epistle, but Arnold has been bothering me in the early part of it, and it is past bedtime now' (*Life and Correspondence of J. D. Coleridge*, i. 129). See also the remarkable tale Miss Margaret Woods tells in the respectable pages of *Essays and Studies by Members of the English Association* (Oxford, 1929, xv. 7–9).
[2] *Life and Correspondence of J. D. Coleridge*, i. 126.

done some business—I have sent our clothes to wash and paid the weekly bill.'[1] Such is the practical value of a Rugby conscience!

Ten days later the situation seems unimproved: 'Matt has gone out fishing, when he ought properly to be working, it being nearly four o'clock . . . it has, however, come on to rain furiously; so Walrond, who is working sedulously at Herodotus, and I, who am writing to you, rejoice to think that he will get a good wetting.'[2]

On November 11, as the examinations draw near, Clough informs Burbidge, 'Matt enters the schools for Paper Work to-morrow. I think he is destined for second; this is above his deserts certainly, but I do not think he can drop below it, and one would not be surprised if he rose above it in spite of all his ignorance. However, he has had the wisdom to be perfectly candid to his doctors as to the amount of the disease and both they and he have been very diligent during the last three weeks.'[3] And seven days later: 'Matt I expect will get a second; he has just concluded his Paper Work. May he also tread in my steps next Easter!'[4]

Arnold did repeat exactly Clough's academic record. The second class at Balliol was followed by a fellowship at Oriel, which he won on Friday, March 28, just thirty years after Dr. Arnold's own election. In the interim he had taught in the lower fifth form at Rugby, as appears from Letter 1. Clough rejoices, of course, that he is now to have him under the same college roof with him: 'First of all, you will be glad to hear that Matt Arnold is elected fellow of Oriel . . . I am only sorry that he will be obliged to leave his present duties at Rugby in Grenfell's place . . . which he appears to have been performing very satisfactorily and with great benefit to himself for the last few weeks. Congreve will go there in three weeks' time; Matt must come into residence as probationary fellow—Mrs. Arnold from whom I have just heard is of course well pleased, as also is the Ven^ble Poet at Rydal who had taken Matt under his special protection as a 2nd classman. I hope it will do

---

[1] Clough MSS.   [2] *Prose Remains*, pp. 95–6.
[3] Clough MSS.   [4] Ibid.

Matt no harm—and he is certainly improved since the disaster of November.' [1]

In 1847 came Arnold's appointment as Lord Lansdowne's private secretary. It is interesting that in a letter, written April 16 of that year, Tom Arnold confides to Clough, 'I quite agree with you in disliking the notion of this appointment for Matt'.[2] There was probably the fear that Lansdowne House, with its splendour and worldliness, would confirm in Arnold tendencies already too manifest. The letters in this book show how powerfully politics, London society, and high affairs attracted him. But they also reveal those other sides of his nature that would have made great houses and public life ultimately unsatisfying. Mrs. Arnold rejoices in 1850, after her son has been over two years with Lord Lansdowne, 'Matt has been with us almost every day since we came up . . . and it is pleasant indeed to see his dear face, and to find him always so affectionate, and so unspoiled by his being so much sought after in a kind of society entirely different from anything we can enter into'.[3] One suspects that, in 1847, not even the family at Fox How or Arthur Clough himself knew how deeply within Matt Arnold streamed the 'buried life'.

II.

The letters themselves take up the tale of Clough's and Arnold's relations after the Oxford days.[4] I have endeavoured, by a running commentary, to make clear, not only the meaning and significance of each separate document, but to introduce new material and to carry a thread of narrative as well. There remains here only the pleasure of considering something of what the letters reveal of Arnold himself and of his ideas.[5]

[1] Clough MSS.—a letter from A. H. C. to J. P. Gell, April 2, 1845. It is partially reproduced in *Prose Remains*, pp. 98–9.
[2] Clough MSS.
[3] *A Writer's Recollections*, p. 46.
[4] Only two of the collection are of the period before Lansdowne House.
[5] I have chosen to discuss here, for the most part, only the *general* aspects of Arnold's later thoughts, the beginnings of which are

'I am forever linked with you by intellectual bonds—the strongest of all', Arnold wrote to Clough, in 1853. The present group of letters, above all else, shows how strong those bonds really were. Drawing out a wealth of ideas upon literature, society, art, and religion, Clough acts upon his friend's mind much as a magnet. It is almost amusing, indeed, to observe how baldly impersonal some of Arnold's notes are. His single pleasure seems to lie in getting certain things *said* to an understanding spirit, who will, in his own turn, bring to the plainest news his own richness and illumination. For friendship, like love, is at bottom the marriage of true minds. Only in that rare alchemy can mere facts begin to breathe, and talk about the King of Prussia, the value of form in poetry, the fate of Clarendon in Ireland, and the changes of Froude's religious thought glow into something almost like sentiment. Then it is that they provide a mutual *causerie* that makes unnecessary those whimsicalities and protestations which are too often the delight of correspondence.

With all the intellectual bias of the letters, however, we constantly get sight of those qualities, which, from a queer habit of divorcing what a person knows from what he is, we like to discriminate as 'the man himself'. Perhaps nowhere do we come closer to Arnold than in his letters from Switzerland, and in the long assurance he gives Clough that an apparent coldness of manner has been but trivial, and no deep alienation. The 'apostle of culture' here, at least, assumes for us some very homely ways. We see the vast transition from the young Rugby master of twenty-two to the Professor of Poetry at Oxford, as early extravagance of expression matures into the manner and style of the *Essays in Criticism*. Seldom does the man depart, even as the years slip by. The young Alpine traveller who loves his 'gossip and the small-wood of humanity' confesses eleven years later, even when he has begun to tell

evidenced in the letters. It must be remembered that he revealed his mind to Clough as he did to no other person except possibly his sister, Jane Forster. It has sometimes seemed convenient to discuss certain topics immediately before or after the letter that raises them, and to show there the relation they have to Arnold's life and work.

31

upon the great world, that were not the results of such a life displeasing, he would willingly fish all day and read the newspapers all the evening, and so live! One sees, too, the familiar dualism that marks the author of *Dover Beach* and of *Friendship's Garland*. The letters are full of banter and the humour of an amused tolerance of the vain shows and absurdities of men. Arnold always seems established at some solid vantage point from which he smiles, but by no means unkindly, at transitory people and at transitory things. His humour is, if closely examined, the humour of *perspective*, in which the eternities laugh at time, the humour of a not unamiable confidence. It is Jove's way, without all of Jove's coldness. The fussy masters of Rugby preserving their pious dignity; the too noble idealism of his brother Tom; the picture of 'his own sinews cracking under the effort to write matter'; the world ducking at the words of professional theologians like half-astonished clowns; the 'funereal solemnity' of two young Oxford scholars doing a translation of Virgil—these are the comedy of life, the critic's comedy. Even in the religious perplexities of 'wandering between two worlds' there is, he implies, something just a bit ridiculous.

The sombre, melancholy strain is there too, however, and it comes from this same critical discernment. Life does not yield for him 'the completeness it suggests'. He reads the Greeks and gains a classical balance that is almost Stoicism, but the romantic in him cannot wholly die. He opens his Goethe, but forgets to close his Byron. He was closer than he knew to much that he disparaged in Keats. For, first of all, he was a poet, and even with the critic's eye he saw a poet's ardent world. No one who expected so little of the gods has more rapturously enjoyed their gifts, or watched more wistfully the certain loss of 'youth and bloom and this delightful world'. The tender view of life he did not cultivate, of course; the war of his maturer years was, indeed, one against low spirits and depression, which 'partake already of the nature of death'. But he could not wholly change his nature.

To few men, moreover, was the *Zeitgeist* a stronger or more dispiriting force. In *The Function of Criticism* and in the essay on Gray, for example, he demonstrates how important to him was the influence of varying epochs. It was the age of prose in which Gray lived, we are told, that choked his poetry and prevented him from speaking out.[1] In like manner Arnold feels himself surrounded by a modern situation that neither Goethe nor Chateaubriand has analysed in its 'true blankness, and barrenness'. 'God keep us from aridity—Arid, that is what the times are!' So from the purer silences of Switzerland he complains of 'the spread of luxury, our physical enervation, the absence of great *natures*, the unavoidable contact with millions of small ones'. Even in the excitement of publishing his own first volume, he bade Clough reflect upon how unpoetical the age and all one's surroundings were—'not unprofound, not ungrand, not unmoving:—but unpoetical'.[2] All this has much to do with a question to be considered somewhat later: namely, why Arnold ceased from poetical performance, at least from any abundance of it, before his life was little more than half over. It is easy enough to say that there is something all too precious and fastidious in this talk against the times; that the true genius will be a law unto himself and, making his own mind a dwelling-place, forget the sense of outward things. His ability to do so, however, will depend entirely on *how* sensitive he is to his milieu. And in larger aspect, is it not perhaps as much a sign of genius to possess an acute sense for *das Gemeine* and the humdrum that binds us all as it is to have an acute sense for beauty and for lights that do not dwell on sea or land? Most great poets have had both senses; and the secret of Arnold's turning from poetry to prose is hardly to be sought in weighing one talent against the other. It lies in a complexity we shall examine somewhat later.

The poet's love of nature, at any rate, is surely his, and in a high degree. The English lakes had taught him as they taught Wordsworth, although by no means the same lessons. The 'nature philosophy' was never his, nor the mysticism that issues from it. Not only from flowers and

[1] *Essays in Criticism*, 2nd series, pp. 69 ff.
[2] See also *Letters*, i. 72–3.

dawns and moving winds was the secret of life to be found,
but chiefly from great men and great books.

> Know, man hath all which Nature hath, but more,
> And in that *more* lie all his hopes of good.

He saw in the world about him not sights and sounds to
charm away the sense, but moral significance—the self-
dependent stars, 'too great for haste, too high for rivalry'.
He also felt and perceived, and often himself attained, that
natural magic for which he praises Keats and Maurice de
Guérin. The letters to Clough have hardly any of the
lavish descriptions that Arnold used to send his mother.
But there is one significant passage, written from Switzerland, in 1848. Complaining of the dirty water he finds
in most of the lakes, he adds, 'The real pain it occasions
to one who looks upon water as the Mediator between
the inanimate and man is not to be described' (No. 22).
Again in 1865, he voices the same dissatisfaction with the
muddy Elbe: 'Now I have a perfect passion for clear water;
it is what in a mountain country gives me, I think, most
pleasure.' I am told also that his consolation for never
being able to visit Greece was the thought that, if he went
at all, it would have to be in summer, when the streams
would all be dry and the journey, therefore, spoiled.

This passion for clear water somehow symbolizes Arnold's
lucid mind and character, his love of simplicity and his
purity of thought and diction. Sainte-Beuve, his master,
had the same affection, and employed in his critiques the
figure of rivers and streams at every chance. It is, in turn,
fascinating to study the theme in Arnold's poems. The
shouts coming across the steaming flats from the far grove
of Mycerinus mix in the still night with 'the murmur of
the moving Nile', which is itself the image of a Necessity
that rolls all things before it. Life is imaged as a river in
A Dream and, more elaborately, in *The Future*, where, upon
the widening course

> the stars come out, and the night-wind
> Brings up the stream
> Murmurs and scents of the infinite Sea.

34

The stream of the *Buried Life*, revealed by love only at moments of rarest insight, sends airs and floating echoes

> From the soul's subterranean depth upborne
> As from an infinitely distant land.

Finally, the Oxus, closing the sad day of Sohrab and Rustum, becomes the majestic image of the fresh start, and then of the shorn and parcelled middle course of the foiled, circuitous wanderer, who hearing finally the longed-for dash of waves, beholds the new-bathed stars emerge and shine upon the Aral Sea. It is like the chorus of a Greek play in its suggestion of human experience and of veritics beyond our reckoning, of some mystery by which 'we feel that we are greater than we know'. It is the supreme expression of Arnold's 'passion for clear water'.

Something of this same clarity of mind and character set him particularly against all influences that distracted him and put him into vain and futile ways of feeling. Deep and long-considered is his protest against newspapers and the idle talk of the day. 'Why do I read about Lord Grey's sending convicts to the Cape, and excite myself thereby, when I can thereby produce no possible good? But public opinion consists in a multitude of such excitements.' Morality was to him just this maintaining of one's integrity, the preserving of one's own essence. By nature, of course, he was a gregarious and many-sided man. If he says to Clough, 'We have the common quality, and rare, of being unambitious', he reveals also how much he was drawn by the great world and high affairs. The careful reader of these letters will see Arnold's constant effort to live by what is permanent, to seek some *principle* by which he can possess his spirit and obtain the clarity that accompanies such poise. His desire, at twenty-seven, is not for 'profound thoughts, mighty spiritual workings, &c., &c., but a distinct seeing of my way as far as my own nature is concerned'. Much as he tries to rouse Clough to some active acceptance of an *assiette* from which to work away, much as he discourages in him the over-questioning spirit, he was himself mightily of Clough's way. The difference between the two, however, was fairly sharp. Clough wished assurance about the eternal verities and certain cosmic truths; Arnold, though he cared for these things too, sought rather some centripetal force by which he could discipline his own diffuse nature. His chief dread was the 'sick hurry, the divided aim'. *Resignation* was written from the heart, from a real Stoicism that had attained no inconsiderable power of renunciation. Long before he became a critic in the literary sense, he became one morally, and the training was not a bad one. The deepest passion of his life was for what is permanent in the human mind and the human heart. 'Die Gestalt dieser Welt vergeht; und ich möchte mich nur mit dem beschäftigen, was bleibende Verhältnisse sind. "The fashion of this world passeth away; and I would fain occupy myself only with the abiding". There is the true Goethe.' And it is the true Arnold, from his early youth to his final hour.

Why then did he virtually turn from poetry? Of all solemn discussions I know, there is none more dull than the debate whether Arnold is greater in poetry than in prose. The real truth is that his efforts in the two fields are *inseparable*, and the reader who knows only one body of his work can hardly say he knows even that. Voices reverberate back and forth between the verse and the essays; the questions raised in one are answered in the other. It is a fair suggestion, in fact, to hold that his poetry and his criticism were never really separate at all. The author of *Memorial Verses, Rugby Chapel, Heine's Grave*, and the *Epilogue to Lessing's Laocoön*, not to mention the sonnets on Shakespeare, Emerson, Sophocles, and the rest, is as distinctly a critic as the author of *Marcus Aurelius, Maurice de Guérin*, and the study of *Celtic Literature* is a poet. Actually the poet in Arnold never died. Oxford engaged him for ten years to lecture on the subject of verse, and he returned to her in *Thyrsis*, one of the richest garlands she has ever worn. It is the poet, moreover, who leads us far beyond Francis Newman and prattling controversy to the real Homeric secrets, and sheds over most of his other literary judgements a warmth and radiance that sets them all apart, each with its own peculiar unction. It is largely because he put his partial, constricted judgement on

36

Shelley into superbly poetic language that it has been so completely remembered and held against him. Even in the most prosaic noon-days of his pamphleteering, the Muse will not desert him; he is concerned over the Burials Bill and Dissenting funerals chiefly because he demands the poetry of Milton in preference to readings from Eliza Cook.[1] Although the critic in him sternly rejects the dogmas of the Catholic Church, he seizes with joy upon its poetry and its rich tradition, suggestive of life that has 'all the pell-mell of the men and women of Shakspeare's plays'.[2]

The letters to Clough particularly reveal how Arnold's critical sense is awakened the moment he has made a verse. In the commentary I have tried to show the significance of what he has to say about the genesis of his own poems and his opinion of them. The conclusion I should draw is, not that his poetic talent was constrained by the critical instinct, but that his output was sharply curtailed by the high standard he set himself. 'Forgive me all this', he adds, after giving Clough's work a severe analysis, 'but I am always prepared to give up the attempt, on conviction: and so, I know, are you: and I only urge you to reflect whether you are advancing.'

The letters suggest other factors which prevented Arnold's work in poetry. To his early conviction that he lived in an unpoetical age was added a more tangible burden. In 1851 he began his work in the schools, with its shiftings from one place to another and its monotony of paper-grading. He expresses his pleasure in writing *Sohrab and Rustum*, only to add that 'it is pain and grief composing with such interruptions as I have'. There is scant evidence whether he also felt that his learning and the really hard study he constantly carried on had sapped his poetic gift and made him receptive rather than creative. The coming publication of his complete note-books will reveal how extensive his reading actually was. In his essay on Gray, with whom he must have felt much in common, he never once suggests, however, that Gray's immense and varied

[1] See *Mixed Essays, &c.*, pp. 404–5.
[2] *Essays in Criticism*, 1st series, pp. 196–7.

37

study hindered his work in poetry. So far as I can recall, he never elsewhere supposes such a thing about himself. But in the letters to Clough he does, and very strongly. Writing in 1849, he numbers among the causes of depression 'the height to which knowledge has come'. Nearly four years later, he tells Clough, in discussing his own poems, 'I feel immensely—more and more clearly what I want— what I have (I believe) lost and choked by my treatment of myself and the studies to which I have addicted myself. But what ought I to have done in preference to what I have done? There is the question.'

Then, too, Arnold was attracted by his natural desire for the attention of a public that, never taking too kindly to his poems, showed a real concern about his prose. New national reviews afforded him a ready medium. Moreover, his trip to the Continent, in 1859, threw him into contact with a whole new set of ideas and interests, and admitted him to a choice circle of foreign critics, including Sainte-Beuve, who also had begun in verse.[1] Lansdowne House, it must be remembered, had taught a zest in politics and public affairs from which he never fully recovered. What

[1] There is, I think, no doubt about Sainte-Beuve's course having had its influence. In Arnold's own copy of *Portraits contemporains* (1847 edition by Didier), he has carefully marked and spent time upon the essay entitled *Dix ans après en littérature*. Here Sainte-Beuve gives a rallying call to criticism, inviting young poets to turn to this other and important art. Surely Arnold must have been thinking of himself as he writes 'rôle de la critique' to mark the following passage: 'La critique est la seconde face et le second temps nécessaire de la plupart des esprits. Dans la jeunesse, elle se recèle sous l'art, sous la poésie; ou, si elle veut aller seule, la poésie, l'exaltation s'y mêle trop souvent et la trouble. Ce n'est que lorsque la poésie s'est un peu dissipée et éclaircie, que le second plan se démasque véritablement, et que la critique se glisse, s'infiltre de toutes parts et sous toutes les formes dans le talent. Elle se borne à le tremper quelquefois; plus souvent elle le transforme et le fait autre. N'en médisons pas trop, même quand elle brise l'art: on peut dire de ce dernier, même lorsqu'il est brisé en critique, que les morceaux en sont bons. Fontenelle nous est un grand exemple; il n'avait été qu'un bel esprit contestable en poésie, un fade novateur évincé; il devint, sous sa seconde forme, le plus consommé des critiques et un patriarche de son siècle. Il y a ainsi, au fond de la plupart des talents, un pis-aller honorable, s'ils savent n'en pas faire fi et comprendre que c'est un progrès.' (p. 527.)

the letters to Clough show, as much as anything else, is the variety of Arnold's concerns. He was destined never to dwell within an ivory tower. Like his father before him, he felt the wider prospect and the relation of all activity. It is a fine bit of irony, I think, that when his first volume of verse was advertised under the initial 'A.' in *The Times* of Monday, February 26, 1849, immediately above it was the notice of the Rev. C. J. Goodhard's *The Lawfulness of Marriage with a Deceased Wife's Sister*. The destinies that turn young poets into pamphleteers must have smiled to themselves that day.

In discussing both Clough's poems and his own, Arnold presents a valuable body of criticism on the subject of poetry in general. Stimulated by the interest he knew that Clough would take in such matters, he goes on to create and express many of those ideas that were later to pass into his essays. One of the chief values of these early opinions is the basis they give for understanding exactly what he meant by saying that poetry was *criticism of life*, a definition which has long been the subject of much comment.

In the first place, Arnold put some restrictions upon his definition that are not always remembered. The criticism must conform always, he says, to the laws of poetic truth and poetic beauty.[1] The high *form* of poetry, its essential element that marks it off from prose;[2] the *architectonicé* which shapes all great works;[3] the distinguished workmanship that makes a small poet such as Gray a memorable one;[4] the necessity of the *beautiful*, in which Emerson, for example, was defective—all these go along with any criticism of life, however profound it may be, before authentic poetry arrives.

Probably because of what he felt were Clough's chief defects as an artist, Arnold stresses the need of form and the need of beauty to a greater degree than he does almost anywhere else. He has 'a growing sense of the deficiency

---

[1] *Essays in Criticism*, 2nd series, pp. 186–7.
[2] *Mixed Essays, &c.*, p. 436.
[3] *Celtic Literature*, p. 79, and *Mixed Essays, &c.*, pp. 496–7.
[4] 'Emerson', *Discourses in America*, p. 157.

39

of the *beautiful*' in his friend's apostrophes to Duty. 'Still, problem as the production of the beautiful remains still to me, I will die protesting against the world that the other is false and jarring.' Form of conception, he insists, is nature's most vital and elemental gift to all born poets, and it must not be risked by going to the bottom of objects at the cost of not *grouping* them. This very form, indeed, is 'the sole *necessary* of poetry, whereas the greatest wealth and depth of matter is merely a superfluity in the Poet *as such*'. The writing of *Sohrab and Rustum* was as congenial a task as he ever performed; but he feels, even so, the lack of 'composition, in the painter's sense'. 'When one thinks of it, our painters cannot *compose* though they can show great genius . . . so too in poetry is it not to be expected that in this same article of *composition* the awkward incorrect Northern nature should show itself?'

We see also here the importance Arnold attaches to metrics and the experiments he tried with them. If his poetry often fails musically, it is his own defect of ear that makes his difficulty, not any neglect of mechanical detail. Like that of Wordsworth, his range of expression is extremely curious and unpredictable. It is a little hard to understand how he who had made the golden cars of Mycerinus 'sweep in the sounding stillness of the night', and uttered the perfect felicities of *Dover Beach*, could have imagined that there was a line of poetry even dormant in

Germany, France, Christ, Moses, Athens, Rome.

Far better, one may say, the Elizabethan extravagance of diction than the armies of exclamation points and jerky phrases that turn Arnold's work at times into a futile sputtering. He could wield the statelier measure in a manner that Milton would not have scorned; and he was not content to rest upon this excellence. As a result, he mars *Thyrsis* with exclamations and deceives himself into thinking that

A prop gave way! crash fell a platform! lo,

could stand as a line of verse. But the slumbers of his Muse are not the fault of any indifference to technique or of failure to appreciate its importance in poetry.

40

His 'criticism of life', then, is not apart from considerations of form and beauty and the power of poetry to furnish pleasure. Yet, while giving these qualities their full place, Arnold did hold that poetry must, in the broadest and highest sense, deal with the question of *how to live*,[1] and that we should 'let our minds rest upon that great and inexhaustible word *life*, until we learn to enter into its meaning. A poetry of revolt against moral ideas is a poetry of revolt against *life*; a poetry of indifference towards moral ideas is a poetry of indifference towards *life*'.

Frank moralist as he is, Arnold hardly meant that poets were merely to provide us with systems and rules of conduct. Their vocation is more than that. It is to *suggest* to us those emotions and attitudes that arise from a penetration of the *centres* of life. The attempts Clough made to 'solve the Universe' were fatiguing and irritating to his friend. But he is warned, in turn, that poets '*must begin with an Idea of the world in order not to be prevailed over by the world's multitudinousness*'. In other words, the poet of abnormalities, who dwells upon the edge of things and submits to be carried where he will, can never, except by accident, give us a criticism of life that is adequate and impressive. He may amuse and entertain us, and give us memorable moments of exotic beauty. Yet he may fail to show us what, curiously enough, Keats, the 'pure poet', has termed

> the great end
> Of Poesy, that it should be a friend
> To soothe the cares, and lift the thoughts of man.

This 'criticism of life' achieves its end, however—and this is a real contribution of the letters—not merely by giving us adequate ideas. It works upon us equally in the effect of its *style*. Just as the presence or absence of the grand style can only be spiritually discerned, so does it reflect the nobility of the poet's mind and character. Milton's sense of his vocation and his effort to be worthy of its grandeur ennobles the very phrasing of *Paradise Lost*.[2] The 'touchstones', moreover, by which Arnold suggests

---

[1] *Essays in Criticism*, 2nd series, p. 144.   [2] Ibid., pp. 63–4.

we may judge poetry are not entities in themselves, as even so rare a critic as Sir Walter Raleigh has insisted upon making them. They are distinguished not merely by a special beauty or wisdom of their own. They are rather marks upon the way, showing to what depth the poet's criticism of life has let him come; the quality of his utterance will but announce in time the quality of his character and meditation. For with Arnold, as with Carlyle, poetry is musical thought, which, only when it goes deep enough, returns in song. It is nothing less than 'the most perfect speech of man, that in which he comes nearest to being able to utter the truth'.[1] The grand style arises only in a noble nature, from out the lasting centres of man's life.

'There are', we are assured, 'two offices of Poetry—one to add to one's store of thoughts and feelings—another to compose and elevate the mind by a sustained tone, numerous allusions, and a grand style. What other process is Milton's than this last, in Comus for instance? There is no fruitful analysis of character, but a great effect is produced. . . . Nay, in Sophocles what is invaluable is not so much his contributions to. psychology and the anatomy of sentiment as the grand moral effects produced by *style*. For style is the expression of the nobility of the poet's character, as the matter is the expression of the richness of his mind: but on men character produces as great an effect as mind.' (Letter 26.)

The man, therefore, who has great poetry working within him profits in a double sense. Even the chance line that has in itself no teaching may set for him some high essential tone. It plays upon his spirit as a benefit, and waits upon him even when he least suspects. It affords him not only the poet's attitude towards the issues of life, but, by the silent ministration of a great style, it directs him inevitably to a new criticism of his own creation. The reader is thus teased into magnanimous feelings and magnificent desires; for him too the fashion of this world begins to drop away and he is left with the abiding. He is given an 'impression habituelle de sérénité et d'aménité qui nous réconcile;

[1] *Essays in Criticism*, 2nd series, p. 128.

nous en avons souvent besoin, avec les hommes et avec nous-même'.[1]

The letters to Clough reveal, in this connexion, how closely Arnold's conception of poetry as a criticism of life is related to his insistence upon a great *subject* and to his belief that Elizabethan literature, with its love of fine writing and beautiful passages, has set us false models. His clearest summary of this view he sends to Clough in October 1852, at the time his ideas were forming for what is in some ways his most important critical utterance, the *Preface to the Poems of 1853*: 'More and more I feel that the difference between a mature and a youthful age of the world compels the poetry of the former to use great plainness of speech as compared with that of the latter: and that Keats and Shelley were on a false track when they set themselves to reproduce the exuberance of expression, the charm, the richness of images, and the felicity of the Elizabethan poets. Yet critics cannot get to learn this, because the Elizabethan poets are our greatest, and our canons of poetry are founded on their works. They still think that the object of poetry is to produce exquisite bits and images—such as Shelley's *clouds shepherded by the slow unwilling wind*, and Keats passim: whereas modern poetry can only subsist by its *contents*: by becoming a complete *magister vitae* as poetry of the ancients did: by including, as theirs did, religion with poetry, instead of existing as poetry only, and leaving religious wants to be supplied by the Christian religion, as a power existing independent of the poetical power. But the language, style, and general proceedings of a poetry which has such an immense task to perform, must be very plain, direct, and severe: and it must not lose itself in parts and episodes and ornamental work, but must press forwards to the whole.' (Letter 40.)

When poets think and feel thus about their vocation they are already critics. One is rather startled to discover, however, that Arnold's turning to prose cost him real effort. 'The Preface is done', he writes Clough in 1853. 'How difficult it is to write prose: and why? Because of

[1] Sainte-Beuve, *Causeries du Lundi*, quatrième édition, iii. 55.

43

the *articulations of the discourse*: one leaps these over in Poetry —places one thought cheek by jowl with another without introducing them and leaves them—but in prose this will not do. It is, of course, not right in poetry either—but we all do it.'

Here we have the secret, I believe, of those repetitions in Arnold's essays, against which so many of his readers have rebelled. He was a schoolmaster and, as such, knew the magnitude of human inattention. It was, therefore, a principle with him to say the same thing several times. But it was also this other self-consciousness about 'articulations in the discourse' that put often in his best work double and triple joints that clinch his meaning to the point of boredom.[1]

Once initiated into prose and the perfecting of his powers, what was the great service that Arnold did for English criticism? I believe it was a double one. He gave it a positive rather than a negative tone; and he broke its provinciality by turning into it the fresh thought of the Continent. The interest Arnold had in France and Germany, and in their important literature, appears continually in these letters. The child-like pleasure he takes in Rapet's praise of his report upon the French schools shows the attraction a wider 'republic of letters' had for him at a time when the bees of English criticism did not roam very far afield to get their honey, and when a smug confidence in English genius was more common than a desire to learn from foreigners. He and Clough shared, as they had in their early Oxford days of attraction by George Sand, the firm conviction that a critic who knew only his own literature did not know even that.

---

[1] It is only fair to remember, however, that Arnold was used to putting quotations in his note-books and reflecting on them repeatedly. This habit made him attach to certain phrases overtones and connotations that escape his reader, who sees these same phrases time and again in the essays. The error was the failure to realize that others had not constructed about these words the same aura of meditation that he had. The grace of God, he believed, often consisted in setting certain thoughts strongly before the mind and in keeping off others. But he forgot that Alcibiades could not tolerate, even from Socrates, the same thing twice.

44

Together with his width of view and desire for fresh horizons, Arnold brought to his critical task the positive enthusiasm for ideas that these letters also display. He established a happy mean between the two schools of criticism that had most dominated England. Patently judicial in his estimates, he has, however, none of the omniscient triumph of the old *Edinburgh* and *Quarterly* reviewers, who either dragged their victims along in a kind of Roman triumph, or else left them lying on the field. And, if he has not quite the rapture and warmth of Hazlitt and Lamb—though something of their enthusiasm he does possess—he escaped, on the other hand, their provincialism and put the critic's business in a larger way.

When I say that Arnold gave a positive tone to English criticism, I do not mean he was not exclusive. He was furiously so. The votaries of Keats and Shelley will be as offended by these letters as they are by his essays.[1] Keats has all the faults of his Elizabethan models and is confused by the multitude of sensations that consume him. Even with his high gift, he 'cannot produce the truly living and moving, as his conscience keeps telling him'. And Arnold's estimate of his contemporaries will always bring upon his head the charge of jealousy. But, even so, he never conceived the business of criticism as the mere massacre of what was bad. The fact that he believed excellence not common never spoiled his joy in looking for it. Sainte-Beuve had taught him the reward of an abundant curiosity. Fresh knowledge was his passion, by which he *forgot* the bad in his delight in new-found good. Rather than convict a Burns of lacking high seriousness, he preferred to come upon a Vinet, a Joubert, a Bishop Wilson, or a Maurice de Guérin and pass them on to others.

There is a striking illustration in the letters of this positive temper of Arnold's, this desire to get the final benefit of all he touches, even while he may exclude a part. One of the important pronouncements in the essays is his belief that Shakespeare, although he is 'the richest, the most wonderful, the most powerful of our writers', is not

[1] Arnold's manuscript note-books reveal that he had planned a second essay on Shelley, which death kept him from completing.

'altogether nor even eminently an *artist*'.[1] On August 3, 1853, he writes to Clough, 'I am beginning the Tempest. How ill he often writes! but how often, too, how incomparably!' Arnold doubtless knew the originality and force of his strictures on Shakespeare at a time when idolatry was the only form of criticism. Yet, he never tried to overdo his line or give it an unwarranted importance. 'Shakespeare frequently had', he said, 'passages in a strain quite false, and which are entirely unworthy of him. But one can imagine his smiling if one could meet him in the Elysian fields and tell him so; smiling and replying that he knew it perfectly well himself, and what did it matter?'[2]

Naturally, a great deal is said to Clough about their contemporaries, and, on the whole, not a great amount of good. The failure in intellectual power which he had always charged against Tennyson had prevented him, so Arnold thought, from being 'a great and powerful spirit in any line—as Goethe was in the line of modern thought, Wordsworth in that of contemplation, Byron even in that of passion'.[3] So here he admits the fatigue he feels at Tennyson's 'dawdling' with the 'painted Shell' of the Universe; and, what is most damning of all, replies to a question of Clough's about a line of *Sohrab and Rustum*, that it is 'rather Tennysonian—at any rate it is not good'. Later, in March 1861, 'Tell Tennyson he is the last person on whom I should have dreamed of inflicting a volume of poems—but I have great pleasure in sending him anything of mine that he really wants to see. You need not add that I care for his productions less and less and am convinced that Alfred de Musset and Henri Heine are far more profitable studies, if we are to study contemporaries at all.'

Browning, who had the most pleasant personal relations with Arnold, comes off but little better. He possesses no idea of the world that supports him centrally and is overcome, as Keats is, by the multitudinousness of life. Arnold can hardly be called jealous of his rival poets, however; for

[1] See *Mixed Essays*, pp. 144, 183, 200, 440 ff., 496 ff.; and *Essays in Criticism*, 2nd series, pp. 62–3.
[2] *Essays in Criticism*, 2nd series, p. 135.
[3] See *Letters*, i, pp. 147, 191, 277–8; ii, p. 10.

he condemns his own work in these letters, and Clough's too, with equally unsparing hand. The simple truth is that he was committed, as few men have ever been, to a rare and high standard, with perhaps too marked a tendency to despise anything that was too near him, including himself. His honest comparison of his own work with that of his rivals is by now familiar: 'It might be fairly urged that I have less poetical sentiment than Tennyson, and less intellectual vigour and abundance than Browning; yet, because I have perhaps more of a fusion of the two than either of them, and have more regularly applied that fusion to the main line of modern development, I am likely enough to have my turn, as they have had theirs.'

Arnold's evolution in his estimate of Carlyle is an interesting study, too. Carlyle's was one of the early voices he heard at Oxford; and these letters show how much Arnold had absorbed. He admires the article on *Louis Philippe*, in 1848, especially 'the style and feeling by which the beloved man appears'. But, by 1859, he mocks 'that regular Carlylean strain which we all know by heart and which the clear-headed among us have so utter a contempt for'. It is in a letter from Switzerland, in the autumn of 1849, however, that he refers to his weariness of 'moral desperadoes like Carlyle'. Apparently he had already become irritated by those defects of *temper*, which he discusses some thirty years later in comparing Carlyle with Emerson. There is also the growing conviction that Carlyle is 'carrying coals to Newcastle' in preaching earnestness to a nation that 'had plenty of it by nature, but was less abundantly supplied with several other useful things'.[1] *Sartor Resartus*, although its peculiar genius had been a tonic force to him, perhaps had offered him no clearer seeing of his way. In the spring of 1848, Clough too, always personally devoted to Carlyle, had said, in bidding Emerson good-bye at Liverpool, 'Think where we are. Carlyle has led us all out into the desert, and he has left us there.' Whereupon, Emerson put his hand upon the other's head, saying, 'Clough, I consecrate you Bishop of all England'. Teufelsdröckh had had his day.

[1] *Letters*, ii. 222.

'Whosoever seriously occupies himself with literature', Arnold once wrote, 'will soon perceive its vital connexion with other agencies.'[1] This vital connexion he not only perceived, but entered into with energy and effect. Quite apart from their chief concern, which is poetry, the letters show glimpses of his first thinking upon politics, society, and religion; they contain practically the first statement of almost every important view he took of life.

The Revolution of 1848, for example, was for him an arresting spectacle. But he senses, amid all the new scheme that is supposedly dawning, that man *restat vivere*, after his plans for an Utopia have all been tried. It is to this *living* side of man that Arnold addresses himself in his social thinking, and in this he sees that man has, beyond his need for bread, two more central needs: the need for culture and the need for righteousness. The letters suggest this recognition. The only political activity that long attracts him is a disinterested and indirect activity that addresses itself to man's deep wants, and in the end becomes the only panacea. When aristocracies have grown impervious to ideas, when the middle classes are immersed in their vulgar self-satisfaction, no machinery will be relieving. Only the slow transforming power of culture, aided by the readier force of state action, can then avail. The collective best-self of a nation once assembled, the individual, too, may then more readily arrive at that fine balance of his powers wherein he becomes a new and better creature.

For Englishmen, Arnold believed that France offered the surest model. Its equality and the general intelligence of its people were exactly what the British Philistine most needed to observe. America, on the other hand, presented only a heightened picture of the Englishman's own faults. What Arnold says in these letters about the United States will seem harsh and rather superficial. It must be remembered, in all fairness, that he enjoys bantering Clough about his boyhood home.[2] But extravagance of statement aside, Arnold deeply believed, and it has done her good to be so reminded, that America fell seriously short in what

[1] *Mixed Essays, &c.*, p. vii.
[2] At Rugby, Clough was often called 'Tom Yankee'.

was beautiful and in what was interesting; that, for all her political conveniences and her material success, she ran the risk of failing 'in whatsoever things were elevated'.[1] At all events, Chicago made a poor study for Englishmen to pursue; for, in the last resort, a 'nation is really civilised by acquiring the qualities it by nature is wanting in'.[2]

On matters of religion, Matthew Arnold has never yet had a proper hearing, because his critics have been unable to believe that he knew much about the subject. It is surprising to observe, in his manuscript note-books, just what the extent of his theological study was. As far as Arnold himself went, of course, he gloried in his deficiencies in theology and formal philosophy. He freely admitted his ignorance in these things, even beyond what it was; for he held this ignorance to be his advantage.

The vague metaphysical jargon of most philosophy left him untouched. With Michelet, he believed it but a method of bewildering oneself methodically. He deplores Amiel's 'vague aspiration and indeterminate desire',[3] upbraids the professional Wordsworthians for giving their poet a 'system',[4] and commends Tolstoy for his lack of abstraction and aridity.[5] He was completely with Joubert who held, 'The true science of metaphysics consists not in rendering abstract that which is sensible, but in rendering sensible that which is abstract; apparent that which is hidden; imaginable, if so it may be, that which is only intelligible; and intelligible, finally, that which an ordinary attention fails to seize'.[6] Like his own Empedocles, he bemoaned the habit of spending all one's wit 'to name what most employ unnamed'.

Likewise, he believed the professional theologian obscured, with his talk of first causes, miracles, and theories of atonement, the real faith he sought to reveal; that the literary man, on the contrary, with his ready tact for essentials, with his trained power of knowing where to rest in a book and where to go lightly, had a definite contribution to make towards a study of the Bible. 'The world in

[1] *Discourses in America*, p. 66.　　　　[2] *Letters*, i. 326.
[3] *Essays in Criticism*, 2nd series, pp. 312–14.　　[4] Ibid., pp. 148 ff.
[5] Ibid., p. 285.　　　　[6] *Essays in Criticism*, 1st series, p. 281.

general', he says to Clough, 'has always stood towards religions and their doctors in the attitude of a half-astonished
clown, acquiescingly ducking at their grand words and
thinking it must be very fine, but for its soul not being able
to make out what it is all about.' And he believes, secondly,
that the religious sentiment is 'best not regarded alone, but
considered in conjunction with the grandeur of the world,
love of kindred, love, gratitude, etc.'

The person familiar with Arnold's religious work will
have recognized that he was already embarked. For his
trouble he was often laughed at or abused. He shocked
some and offended others. But, when the final history of
nineteenth-century thought is written, he will be credited,
one may fairly assume, with a distinguished service. And
his service was to show men that their faith eventually
rested, not on the doubtful science of a Book which was
never intended to be scientific, but upon the everlasting
moral truths that Book reveals, and as they are nowhere
else revealed. It was to draw the gaze of many a common
man from a sick dismay at the blind quarrels of the doctors,
and to fix his attention upon righteousness and the joy that
arises from that; to let him find the Bible was, in every
sense, again the living word; to open to him the way of
renunciation; to show him once more the sweet reasonable-
ness of Jesus and His promise that He was meek and lowly
at heart, and that He would give us rest unto our souls.

Perhaps the most startling thing about the letters to
Clough is their revelation that, even in his late twenties, in
the period from 1848 to 1853, in which one thinks of Arnold
as rather far removed from any religious certainty, he had
already set his course and caught the significance of what
he later was to teach others. He tells us, too, who his helper
was. It was Spinoza, with his 'positive and vivifying atmosphere', demanding 'What! our knowledge of God to
depend upon these perishable things, which Moses can
dash to the ground and break to pieces like the first tables
of stone, or of which the originals can be lost like the original
book of the Covenant, like the original book of the Law of
God, like the book of the Wars of God! . . . which can come
to us confused, imperfect, mis-written by copyists, tampered

with by doctors! and you accuse others of impiety! It is you who are impious, to believe that God would commit the treasure of the true record of himself to any substance less enduring than the heart!' He who has mastered this thought of Spinoza and followed its ramifications has mastered half the religious teaching of Matthew Arnold. The other half is Jesus Christ, his perfect temper, his perfect intuition.

What will be Matthew Arnold's claim upon the future? It will be a varied one, and it cannot be predicted safely now. But one claim he has already, one merit by which he stands almost alone in the field of English letters. More than any other of his contemporaries, he comes to us as the symbol of that quality which he himself believed would some day save the world—the quality that arises from the union of reason with imagination.

Imagination is not uncommon, and reason less scarce than we sometimes think. But the blend of these two is another thing and still rare enough to be distinguished. The Victorian compromise, we are told, was in the struggle between fanatical rationalism, on the one hand, and fanatical religion, on the other. In Arnold we see both these extremes making their demands, but neither given any place. For what commonly passes as mysticism he has no quarter; he seeks only those outposts that are 'perfectly in light and firm'. Tennyson's music cannot charm him away, and Browning's buoyant faith he cannot follow. He only *thinks* he knows

> The hills where his life rose,
> And the sea where it goes.

Yet, out of his own integrity, he heightens reason until it becomes itself transformed and includes some deeper quality of the soul. Upon the shelves of his study is Voltaire in seventy volumes, and near to him Saint Francis of Assisi. One month he studies Locke and, another, the Benedictine Rule. Into his pocket diaries he puts one day a cynical *mot* of La Bruyère or La Rochefoucauld, and next day he enters, 'Blessed are the pure in heart, for they shall see God.' He loved the forum and the

51

market-place and pagan scholarship; but out of his secret meditation and the long quiet of his daily reading, he has compiled for us one of the great devotional books of the world. By a happy sequence, he who all his life was the foe of sentimentality and excessive feeling is, so complete was his unction, the one man of his time who insists that it is only the accent of deep *emotion* that raises morality into religious joy and marks the difference between the two. It is because he owns, in the far range of his life and work, this rare balance of opposing qualities that we can give him first our confidence; and, by this same balance, he gives light and leading to a time that needs it more perhaps than did his own.

For a man of sanity and caution he has said at times some foolish things. We shall continue to correct his judgements about French poetry, and Keats, and Shelley, and the Celts, and marriage with a deceased wife's sister. Closing the *Stanzas from the Grande Chartreuse* and feeling his power as an artist, we shall weep momentarily for the folly of the poet who left his vocation and went round begging the British Philistine to become urbane and civilized. We shall smile at his fine airs and his grand ways. We shall deplore his dogmatism, which he himself said was different from that of Mr. Ruskin, because Mr. Ruskin was sometimes *wrong*! But all this coming to pass, Arnold will still have his deeper meaning undisturbed. He rests ultimately upon a distinguished principle of life that is beyond all tiny cavil.

The word *adequate* was to him a word of high significance. Because he gives us, not one thing, but two, and these not separately; because he shows us the fruitful marriage of reason and imagination, his favoured word becomes his praise. As these letters fully show, he moved along a *via media* into a new life, towards that central quiet of the spirit which is the sign and seal of all abiding things, and 'being one with which we are one with the whole world'.

In the friend of *Thyrsis* he had one who was exactly like him in the things that matter much. 'It is to Arnold and Clough,' a distinguished critic has told us, 'that the men of the future will come who desire to find the clearest expression of the most cultivated and thoughtful men of our generation.' They will find something more perhaps; for the best that Arnold and Clough afford will not be a mere record of the far way and long ago. Both of them present a living faith in what is excellent, for it was clearly the common motive of their lives. It is this faith that marks a little company of rare spirits who will be for ever precious to mankind. As long as they shall last

Our Tree yet crowns the hill,
Our Scholar travels yet the loved hill-side.

LETTERS

I

[The youthful, exuberant letter which begins this collection was written during the early part of 1845. Arnold was teaching classics at Rugby, in the lull between his taking second class at Balliol and his winning the Oriel Fellowship. Dr. Tait, then head master, had engaged him to assist with the fifth form. He won the Oriel honour on March 28. The context shows that this letter was written shortly before that date.

Clough was, of course, at Oriel; Tom Arnold, at University College; and Theodore Walrond, the close friend of both Clough and the Arnolds, at Balliol.

The satire on Tractarianism and academic pomposity foreshadows, for all its verbiage and excessive spirit, the future castigator of the Philistines. The reference to 'patent simulators' suggests that Carlyle has already had his way with Arnold and is here probably inspiring the euphuistic outburst.]

Rugby. Wednesday.
[shortly before March 28, 1845]

My dear Clough

Your letters touched on business, and therefore tho: one is lost, I will try and say something. First my love to Walrond, with a reference to the Corner of the 11th Page of my 7th Tract—where he will find that 'the Rewards of intellectual ambition are at best transitory: but a quiet Conscience is an unfailing Friend'. He being thus soothed, and Tom being waived, as surely written in my heart, and Pits, as surely soon to be written to with Paper and Ink, let me say that a faint Image of my present Labours may be shadowed forth under the Figure of Satan, perambulating, under the most unfavourable circumstances, a populous neighbourhood thro: which I have lately passed distributing Tracts: which reminds me that I do not give satisfaction at the Masters Meetings. For the other day when Tait had well observed that strict Calvinism devoted 1000s of mankind to be eternally,—and paused—I, with, I trust the true Xtian Simplicity suggested '——'. Which was yet nothing to that plainer saying of P. Arnolds[1] at the same

55

meeting, when, disparaging the Qualifications of Mayor as a Master, and ungenerously taunting him with an inborn stiffness of carriage, he remarked that 'Hell fire would not make him dance'.—

—But you are not to suppose that these Druidical Remains, these touches, if I may so speak, of the aboriginal Briton, are found often among the stately Edifices of our Magistracy: nor yet are you not to suppose that it is so late at night that this licentious Pen wanders whither it will. True, I give satisfaction—but to whom? True, I have yet been late on no Morning, but do I come behind in no thing? True, I search the Exercises, but the Spirits? —For which Reason it seems not clear why I should stand at Oriel: for wisdom I have not, nor skilfulness—after the Flesh—no, nor yet Learning: and [who] will see a delicate Spirit tossed on Earth, opossum like, with the down fresh upon him, from the maternal Pouches of nature, in the grimed and rusty coalheaver, sweating and grunting

> with the Burden of an honour
> Unto which he was not born.—

I have other ways to go. But you may tell Congreve[2] as to the stabling—that is not the business: but the Business is between us two, and I feel his kindness. I hear a huge form, the Lower 5th. He will get a hundred Pounds from Easter till June. He is free on the 28th of June. Till then he lodges not takes Possession: would the Varlet push dying Men from their Stools? And the same to you.

—But, my dear Clough, have you a great Force of Character? That is the true Question. For me, I am a reed, a very whoreson Bullrush: yet such as I am, I give satisfaction. Which you will find to be nothing—nor yet is a patent Simulation open to all men, nor to all satisfactory. But to be listless when you should be on Fire: to be full of headaches when you should slap your Thigh: to be rolling Paper Balls when you should be weaving fifty Spirits into one: to be raining when you had been better thundering: to be damped with a dull ditchwater, while in one school near you sputters and explodes a fiery tailed Rocket, and in the rest patent Simulators ceaselessly revolve: to be all

this, and to know it—O my Clough—, in this house they
find the Lodger in Apricot Marmalade for two meals a day
—and yet?—But, my love, the clock reminds me that I
long since sung,

'Night comes:—with Night comes Silence, hand in hand:—
With Night comes Silence, and with that, Repose:—
And pillows on her frozen breast, and locks
Within the Marble Prison of her arms
The 'Usher's' rash and feverish Melancholy:
Cuts short the Feignings of fantastic Grief,
Freezes the sweet strain on the parted Lips,
And steals the honied Music of his Tongue—[3]
—Which last two Lines, I perceive, hang loosely around
the Point. In drowsiness and heaviness, Goodnight, and
love to all.

> ever yours lovingly
> M. ARNOLD.—

[1] Charles Thomas Arnold, nicknamed 'plug', was a friend of Clough,
both at Rugby and at Oxford. He returned to his old school in 1841,
where he served as master until his death in 1878. His disparaging
remarks were cast at Charles Mayor, assistant master. (See *Rugby
School Register, 1675–1867*, p. 101.)

[2] Richard Congreve (1818–99), the English Positivist, came to
Rugby as assistant master in 1845. For an interesting appreciation of
his ability as a teacher, see Frederic Harrison, *Autobiographic Memoirs*,
Macmillan, London, 1911, i. 83 ff.

[3] This is a partial burlesque of one of Arnold's own early verses that
appears among a collection of notes towards his poems, the manuscript
of which is in possession of Professor C. B. Tinker, of Yale University.
Throughout these letters Arnold frequently quotes his own lines.
Some of them are part of his published work; others are doubtless, like
this one, discarded fragments.

<hr>

2

[In spite of its abrupt beginning, the manuscript of this letter
seems not to be a fragment. The contents do not determine
a definite date. However, the style, the handwriting, and the
enthusiastic references to George Sand certainly make it fall
within the Oxford period prior to Arnold's entry at Oriel.
It very likely was written from Rugby, about the same time
as the previous letter. It can hardly be later than 1845.

While Arnold was at Balliol, he and Clough conceived a

passion for George Sand's novels (see Introduction, p. 20). This letter shows that Arnold's joy in reading lay partly in the shock he gave his more conventional friends, to whom Mrs. Trimmer's 'edifying' treatises or Hannah More's aphorisms were better fare.

Indiana, George Sand's first independent novel, contains a letter from Indiana to Raymon, her former lover, which is a passionate statement of a free, non-conforming religious idealism. Apparently it affected Arnold deeply. Much of it he quotes from memory. So important is this passage in what it tells us indirectly about his early thinking that it has seemed well to give much of the original French text in Appendix III (see p. 167). The parts Arnold here translates are there included. The verse that begins his own letter is little more than a paraphrase of George Sand's sentiment. The 'Sunday shoes letter' from *Jacques* follows Indiana's letter in the same appendix.

The praise of George Sand, amplified later in Arnold's essay on her, did not come averse to Clough, although he had more moderate appreciation. To his friend Burbidge, on October 28, 1845, he confesses, 'I have however found time in the last three days to read "Jeanne par George Sand", the most cleanly French novel I ever read—and not cleanly only but pure. What one has heard of the actual life of Mad. Du-devant is certainly, so far as it goes, against her in this respect. Howbeit I incline to believe her a Socrates among the Sophists.' Clough MSS.]

[See introductory note, p. 57, for date]

Ye too, who stand beside the hoary Throne,
Where Time, else dumb, hath signified his Sway,
To the blind slaves of Power to make it known
Material Grandeurs do in Heaven decay,
—Keep all, o keep, continual holiday!
And let—&c

— w[hi]ch whence it proceeds you do not know: You mean INDIANA's LETTER, without which I think the book not preeminent among the Author's other novels. 'Believe me', (I quote from Memory)—'if a Being so vast deigned to take any Part in our miserable Interests, it would be to raise up the weak, and to beat down the strong:—it would be to pass his heavy hand over our heads, and to level them like the waters of the Sea:—to say to the Slave, "Throw away thy chain",—and to the Strong, "Bear thy Brother's burden: for I have given him strength and wisdom, and thou shalt oppress him no longer." '—And the correspondence of Jacques and Sylvia—the Sunday Shoes letter you remember. But never without a Pang do I hear of the growing Popularity of a strong minded writer. Then I know what hideosities what Solecisms, what Lies, what crudities, what distortions, what Grimaces, what affectations, what disown[m]ents of that Trimmer-X-Hannah-More-typed spirit they are of, I shall hear and see amongst the born-to-be-tight-laced of my friends and acquaintance: then I know the strong minded writer will lose his self-knowledge, and talk of his usefulness and imagine himself a Reformer, instead of an Exhibition. Rightly considered, a Code-G.-Sand would make G. Sands impossible.[1] The true world for my love to live in is, a general Torpor, with here and there a laughing or a crying Philosopher. And whilst my misguided Relation[2] exchanges the decency God dressed his Features in for the déshabille of an Emotee, we, my love,[3] lovers of one another and fellow worshippers of Isis, while we believe in the Universality of Passion as Passion, will keep pure our Aesthetics by remembering its onesidedness as doctrine. Oh my love suffer me to stop a little. —Very much later, almost night. Oh my love, goodnight.

                             M. ARNOLD.—

[1] What Arnold probably means is that George Sand's fresh and living views of society, if hardened into law, would at once lose their vital freedom and play.

[2] The 'misguided Relation' is most likely Tom Arnold, who already at Oxford was revealing the tendencies that turned him to the Roman Church.

[3] This curious expression, which might lead some to think the unaddressed letter was really not for Clough at all, but for some lost 'Marguerite', occurs in other letters in this collection, as well as in other parts of Clough's correspondence.

3

[The date of this letter can be fairly well postulated by reference to letter No. 5, which shows that in late November and early December 1847 Arnold had been reading the manuscript of Clough's verses. The present, obviously written about the

same time of year, gives Arnold's opinion of one of those
poems. It seems logical, therefore, to fix the date of this criticism
as 1847, in Arnold's first winter in London as secretary to
Lord Lansdowne. Clough is still at Oriel.]

London. Wednesday.

[late November—early December 1847?]

Dear Clough

Till Tuesday in next week I shall certainly be here, and
probably longer.—Blackett[1] wants me to pass the Nativity
of our B. L. with him and his sister at Brighton. But I am
not earnestly bent on this.—You talked of coming here on
the 7th—Why not now till Saturday?—Everything in its
own order as Paul or Peter observes. The 7 Spirits Poem[2]
does well what it attempts to do I think. Tho: I still ask
why 7. This is the worst of the allegorical—it instantly in-
volves you in the unnecessary—and the unnecessary is
necessarily unpoetical. Goly what a Shite's oracle! But
profoundly true.—Besides its trueness to its purpose, or
constituting this, the feeling is deep in the Poem, and
simul[taneously] runs clear. Farewell David. Had I the
skill I had e'er Rudge flitted wormwards I would limn
Bathsheba washing herself.—Bring up my gold in the
paniers of an ass. I spell *paniers* so.

M. ARNOLD.

[1] John F. B. Blackett, a mutual friend of Arnold and Clough, was
then in London. From 1852 to 1856 he sat as member for Newcastle.
[2] *The Questioning Spirit* (see Clough's *Poems*, Macmillan, London,
1913, p. 185). The early manuscript note-book that contains the first
draft does have the seven spirits which make for the confusion Arnold
suggests. As to his distaste for allegory in poetry see also his 'A French
Critic on Milton' and his 'Preface to the Poems of 1853', *Mixed Essays,
&c.*, pp. 196 and 495: ' "A true allegory of the state of one's own mind
in a representative history," the poet is told, "is perhaps the highest
thing that one can attempt in the way of poetry." . . . No, assuredly,
it is not, it never can be so: no great poetical work has ever been
produced with such an aim.'

———

4

[This is clearly the 'beastly vile note' for which Arnold
apologizes a few days later in the letter that follows it, of
mid-December 1847.

Clough was considering then the verses he might include in

a joint publication with his old school-friend, Thomas Burbidge. Their *Ambarvalia* did not appear, however, until a year later, partly because in September 1848 Clough was sidetracked by an inspiration for his long-vacation poem, *The Bothie of Toper-na-fuosich.*

Arnold refers to two manuscript note-books in the present Clough collection. One of them contains fair copies of poems written from 1839 to 1842; the other, later verses.]

My dear Clough   [London, early December 1847]

I have had so much reluctance to read these, which I now return that I surely must be destined to receive some good from them.

—I have never been reminded of Wordsworth in reading them by rhythms or expressions: but of Tennyson sometimes and repeatedly of Milton—Little hast thou bested etc, e.g,[1] sounds to me Miltonically thought and expressed.

I have abstained from all general criticism, but here and there put a word agst an expression: but as it was done at a first reading, these are to be very slightly attended to.—
It would amuse you to see how treatments differ, if you saw some things in which I have come on the same topics as you: those of your 4th poem. 1st vol. e.g.[2]

—The 2nd Poem in the 1st volume[3] I do not think—valuable—worthy of you—what is the word?
—And as a metrical curiosity the one about 2 musics[4] does not seem to me happy.

But on the whole I think they will stand very grandly, with Burbidge's 'barbaric ruins' smirking around them. I think too that they will give the warmest satisfaction to your friends who want to see something of yours. Stanley will have the 'calf'[5] one by heart the day it appears. If I cannot come and see you, I will try to write.

               Yours
               M. ARNOLD.

From *In a Lecture-Room*:
> Away, haunt thou not me
> Thou vain Philosophy!
> Little hast thou bestead
> Save to perplex the head,
> And leave the spirit dead.

² The 4th poem in the copy-book is:

Like a child
In some strange garden left awhile, alone,
I pace about the pathways of the world
Plucking light hopes and joys from every bough,
With qualms of vague misgivings in my heart
That payment in the end will be required,
Payment I cannot make, or guilt incurred
And shame to be endured.

For later draft, see *Poems*, p. 14.

Although Arnold's *Religious Isolation* suggests the same theme, I believe he has in mind his *To a Gipsy Child by the Sea-shore*, wherein the infant's pensive, misgiving face predicts the matured Stoic who 'ere the long evening close' shall return and 'wear this majesty of grief again'. It is interesting to find that Arnold, his mother, and his sister were spending the vacation in the Isle of Man, the scene of the poem, in the summer of 1845. (See *The Correspondence of Henry Crabb Robinson with the Wordsworth Circle*, ii. 609.)

³ It is the one beginning:

Enough, small Room: tho' all too true
Much ill in thee I daily do.

Perhaps Arnold recalled unpleasant memories of Tennyson's 'darling room'. Clough never printed his poem.

⁴ *The Music of the World and of the Soul*, the second stanza of which begins 'Are there not, then, two musics unto men?'

⁵ Arthur Stanley's admiration is predicted for what is later entitled *The New Sinai*.

5

[A fairly definite date can be assigned this letter. Tom Arnold sailed for New Zealand on November 24, 1847, from Gravesend, in the steamer *John Wickliffe*. He describes the storms at the outset of his voyage down the Channel during 'the wintry gloom of a British December' (see his *Passages in a Wandering Life*, pp. 65–6). One of the worst hurricanes that ever swept England played havoc with all shipping from Saturday, December 4, until the middle of the following week. The newspapers contained special articles on the loss of life and property. See London *Times*, Dec. 6–9, and *Examiner*, Dec. 11, 1847, p. 796, which devotes three-fourths of a column to the disasters.

Arnold softens his criticism of the previous note, although he gives the frank opinions that throughout these letters characterize his attitude toward Clough and his work. The 'apostrophes to duty' that set him on edge were roughly scribbled stanzas in a manuscript note-book for 1839–42, beginning 'Duty—that's to say, complying'. *Poems*, p. 181.]

[London]
[shortly after December 6, 1847]

My dear Clough

I sent you a beastly vile note the other day: but I was all rasped by influenza and a thousand other bodily discomforts. Upon this came all the exacerbation produced by your apostrophes to duty: and put me quite wrong: so that I did not at all do justice to the great precision and force you have attained in those inward ways. I do think however that rare as individuality is you have to be on your guard against it—you particularly:—tho: indeed I do not really know that I think so. Shakspeare says that if imagination would apprehend some joy it comprehends some bringer of that joy: and this latter operation which makes palatable the bitterest or most arbitrary original apprehension you seem to me to despise. Yet to *solve* the Universe as you try to do is as irritating as Tennyson's dawdling with its painted shell [1] is fatiguing to me to witness: and yet I own that to *re-construct* the Universe is not a satisfactory attempt either—I keep saying, Shakspeare, Shakspeare, you are as obscure as life is: [2] yet this unsatisfactoriness goes against the poetic office in general: for this must I think certainly be its end. But have I been inside you, or Shakspeare? Never. Therefore heed me not, but come to what you can. Still my first note was cynical and beastly-vile. To compensate it, I have got you the Paris diamond edition of Beranger, like mine. Tell me when you are coming up hither. I think it possible Tom may have trotted into Arthur's Bosom in some of the late storms; which would have been a pity as he meant to enjoy himself in New Zealand. [3] It is like your noble abstemiousness not to have shown him the Calf Poem: he would have worshipped like the children of Israel. Farewell.   yours most truly

M. ARNOLD

[1] For other comments upon Tennyson, see pp. 46, 47, 97, 147, 154.
[2] This passage is interesting because it is really Arnold's own paraphrase of his sonnet on Shakespeare.
[3] Tom Arnold had gone out to New Zealand in a high idealism,

attracted by descriptions of unexplored country and by the setting for 'some kind of Pantisocracy, with beautiful details and imaginary local establishments such as Coleridge never troubled himself to formulate . . .' (*Passages in a Wandering Life*, pp. 64–5.)

6

[There is a question whether the two letters that follow are separate fragments or parts of the same letter. The break in the first manuscript without a period to end the concluding sentence, and the differences in the paper and the handwriting between the two sheets suggest that they were written at different times and with different pens.

On the other hand, the first sheet, by its tearing shows that it was never part of a folder. And the numbering at the top of the second sheet, the only instance of its kind in the whole correspondence, could well imply that it goes with a first and somewhat different looking piece of paper.

For lack of positive evidence to the contrary, the letters are here printed as two fragments. They both are closely related in subject-matter, following logically the discussion of Clough's poems in the previous letters. Arnold apparently acknowledges Clough's reply to the letter of apology written about the middle of December (see letter No. 5).

For Arnold's discussion of poetry and style, see pp. 41–3.]

London. Tuesday.
[December 1847; or early part of 1848]

My dearest Clough

My heart warms to the kindness of your letter: it is necessity not inclination indeed that ever repels me from you.

I forget what I said to provoke your explosion about Burbidge: au reste, I have formed my opinion of him, as Nelson said of Mack.[1] One does not always remember that one of the signs of the Decadence of a literature, one of the factors of its decadent condition indeed, is this—that new authors attach themselves to the poetic expression the founders of a literature have flowered into, which may be *learned* by a sensitive person, to the neglect of an inward poetic life. The strength of the German literature consists in this—that having no national models from whence to get an idea of *style* as half the work, they were thrown upon themselves, and driven to make the fulness of the content

64

of a work atone for deficiencies of form. Even Goethe at
the end of his life has not the inversions, the taking tour-
menté style we admire in the Latins, in some of the Greeks,
and in the great French and English authors. And had
Shakspeare and Milton lived in the atmosphere of modern
feeling, had they had the multitude of new thoughts and
feelings to deal with a modern has, I think it likely the
style of each would have been far less *curious* and exquisite.
For in a *man* style is the saying in the best way *what you have
to say*.[2] The *what you have to say* depends on your age. In
the 17th century it was *a smaller harvest than now*, and sooner
to be reaped: and therefore to its reaper was left time to
stow it more finely and curiously. Still more was this the
case in the ancient world. The poet's matter being *the
hitherto experience of the world, and his own*, increases with every
century. Burbidge lives quite beside the true poetical life,
under a little gourd. So much for him. For me you may
often hear my sinews cracking under the effort to unite
matter. . . .

[1] 'General Mack was at the head of the Neapolitan troops;—all
that is now doubtful concerning this man is, whether he was a coward
or a traitor;—at that time he was assiduously extolled as a most
consummate commander to whom Europe might look for deliverance
. . . but when the general, at a review, so directed the operations of a
mock fight, that, by an unhappy blunder, his own troops were surrounded instead of those of the enemy, he [Nelson] turned to his
friends and exclaimed, with bitterness, that the fellow did not understand his business. . . . "General Mack," said he, in one of his letters,
"cannot move without five carriages! I have formed my opinion.
I heartily pray I may be mistaken".' Southey, *Life of Nelson*, Every-
man edition, chapter 6, p. 137.

[2] G. W. Russell recalls, 'Mr. Matthew Arnold once said to me,
"People think that I can teach them style. What stuff it all is! Have
something to say, and say it as clearly as you can. That is the only
secret of style".' *Collections and Recollections by One Who has kept a
Diary*, Harper, New York and London, 1898, p. 136.

7

[See introductory note to Letter 6, p. 64.

The date of this fragment is set by the reference to the outbreak of the Revolution of 1848 at Paris, to which Arnold
again recurs in the letter that follows this. Louis Philippe was

forced to abdicate on February 24, after several exciting days in which the main question was whether the National Guard would side with the people or break up the reform banquets in the name of the King. The defection of the Guard was the immediate cause of the overturn.]

[London, about February 24, 1848]

A growing sense of the deficiency of the *beautiful* in your poems, and of this alone being properly *poetical*[1] as distinguished from rhetorical, devotional or metaphysical, made me speak as I did. But your line is a line: and you have most of the promising English verse-writers with you now: Festus[2] for instance. Still, problem as the production of the beautiful remains still to me, I will die protesting against the world that the other is false and JARRING.

No—I doubt your being an *artist*: but have you read Novalis?[3] He certainly is not one either: but in the way of direct communication, insight, and report, his tendency has often reminded me of yours, though tenderer and less systematic than you. And there are the sciences: in which I think the passion for truth, not special curiosities about birds and beasts, makes the great professor.—

—Later news than any of the papers have, is, that the National Guard have declared against a Republic, and were on the brink of a collision with the people when the express came away.

—I trust in God that feudal industrial class as the French call it, you worship, will be clean trodden under. Have you seen Michelet's characterisation (superb) of your brothers[4]—'La dure inintelligence des Anglo-Americains.' —Tell Edward I shall be ready to take flight with him the very moment the French land, and have engaged a Hansom to convey us both from the possible scene of carnage.[5]

—yours

M. A.

[1] For Arnold's ideas on poetry, see p. 39 *et seq.* It is worth observing here that the insistence on the *beautiful* as that which is properly *poetical* is remembered even in his later treatment of poetry as a 'criticism of life'. For this criticism of life proceeds under the 'conditions fixed for such a criticism by the laws of poetic truth and poetic beauty'. ('The Study of Poetry', *Essays in Criticism*, 2nd series, p. 5.)

This last part of Arnold's definition is too seldom remembered. The strictures he here makes against Clough are much like those to which he later subjects the poetry of Emerson (*Discourses in America*, pp. 150–9).

² *Festus*, the twenty-thousand line poem by Philip James Bailey, appeared in 1839, and had a wide sale. It is based upon the Faust legend.

³ Arnold had doubtless been attracted to Novalis by his early reading of Carlyle.

⁴ Clough's early boyhood had been spent in Charleston, South Carolina.

⁵ Edward Arnold, Matthew's younger brother, was then at Balliol College. During the whole of January and February 1848 London had been stirred by alarmists about the prospect of a French invasion, the weakness of the national defences having been pointed out by the Duke of Wellington and others. When the crisis at Paris came, England was naturally nervous about the result. (See the first article in the *Examiner* for that year, issue of Saturday, January 1, for a good account of the situation.)

8

[The French Revolution of 1848 aroused a rapid exchange of letters between Arnold and Clough, and stimulated their thinking for the next four months. Lord Lansdowne's secretary naturally felt the excitement in governmental circles. And Clough, the 'Republican Friend' addressed in Arnold's sonnets, far more enthusiastic in his hope for some radical change, wrote to John Campbell Shairp, 'If it were not for all these blessed revolutions, I should sink into hopeless lethargy'. Clough MSS.; letter of March ?, 1848.

On Friday, March 10, 1848, Arnold wrote to his sister Jane: 'My excuse for not answering you, dear child, must be that not having been privately disposed lately, it mattered little. I thought, to whom my public general chronicles or remarks were addressed. . . . It is so hard to sequester oneself here from the rush of public changes and talk and yet so unprofitable to attend to it. I was myself tempted to attempt some political writing the other day, but in the watches of the night I seemed to feel that in that direction I had some enthusiasm of the head perhaps, but no profound stirring. So I desisted, and have only poured forth a little to Clough, we too agreeing like two lambs in a world of wolves. I think you would have liked to see the correspondence.' *Letters*, i. 5, 6. The 'correspondence' includes the next four letters of this series.

The present letter refers to the 'news' of the National
Guard previously cited. The 'Wednesday' date is March 1,
1848. The Poet at the head of the new Provisional Government is Lamartine, who had completely dominated the
situation after February 24.]

London. Wednesday. [March 1, 1848]

My dear Clough

I received yours just now, as I was beginning to drop into
a slight doze over the works and days of the respectable
Hesiod: a result however I attribute not so much to that
writer, as to one St. Marc Girardin, a lecture of whom
upon 'le Caractère du Père dans la Comédie'—I had just
previously closed, one of my painfullest follies being the
itch to read thro: a book whereof I need a small part.

As to my news Lord L[ansdowne] told it me, and it came
from a Govt. messenger—who seems however to have
shared the cock-and-bull—prolific excitement of common
men at these moments. Yesterday I taxed the hoary Com-
municator: and he owned that the assertion was premature:
but declared that numbers of Gig-owners[1] were entering
the N[ational] G[uard] in that view: and instanced the
duc de Guiche. However I think Gig-owning has received
a severe, tho: please God, momentary blow: also, Gig-
owning keeps better than it re-begins. Certainly the present
spectacle in France is a fine one: mostly so indeed to the
historical swift-kindling man, who is not over-haunted by
the pale thought, that, after all man's shiftings of posture,
restat vivere. Even to such a man revolutions and bodily
illnesses are fine anodynes when he is agent or patient
therein: but when he is a spectator only, their kind effect
is transitory.

—Don't you think the eternal relations between labour
and capital the Times twaddles so of[2] have small existence
for a whole society that has resolved no longer to live by
bread alone. What are called the fair profits of capital
which if it does not realize it will leave it's seat and go elsewhere, have surely no absolute amount, but depend on
the view the capitalist takes of the matter. If the rule is—
everyone must get all he can—the capitalist understands
by fair profits such as will enable him to live like a colossal

Nob: and Lancashire artisans knowing if they will not let him make these, Yorkshire artisans will, tacent and sweat. But an apostolic capitalist willing to live as an artisan among artisans may surely divide profits on a scale undreamed of Capitalisto nobefacturo. And in a country all whose capitalists were apostolic, the confusion a solitary apostle would make, could not exist.

—Answer me that. If there is necessity anywhere, it is in the Corruption of man, as Tom might say, only.—

—Burns is certainly an artist *im*plicitly[3]—fury is not incompatible with artistic form but it becomes *lyric* fury (Eh?) only when combined with the gift for this. And Beranger both in—and ex. They accuse him by his finisht classicality of having banished the old native French Forms. O, you must like him.

I wish you could have heard me and my man sneering at the vulgar officiousness of that vulgar fussy Yankee Minister[4] at Paris. My man remarks that Poets should hold up their heads now a Poet is at the head of France. More clergyman than Poet, tho: and a good deal of cambric handkerchief about that. No Parson Adams.[5]

—I am disappointed the Oriental wisdom,[6] God grant it were mine, pleased you not. To the Greeks, foolishness.

Yours
M. A.

[1] This letter admirably illustrates Arnold as 'a liberal tempered by experience', even, indeed, before he had had much experience at all. His reference to Gig-owning as symbolic of the aristocrats is probably inspired by the remarkable use made of the word at the very close of Carlyle's *French Revolution*, when Cagliostro, in his wild, prophetic utterance, sees all the Gigs of Creation going down in the general welter of the world as Imposture is consigned to the flames. The new revolt in France has turned Arnold's mind back on Carlyle's work.

On March 7, 1848, he wrote his mother, 'Still the hour of the hereditary peerage and eldest sonship and immense properties has, I am convinced, as Lamartine would say, struck'. But three days later, he reminds his sister, 'I do not say that these people in France have much dreamed of the deepest wants of man, or are likely to enlighten the world much on the subject.' (*Letters*, i. 5 and 7.)

[2] For the interesting quotation that explains Arnold's discussion, see Appendix IV, p. 169.

[3] The reference to Burns and Béranger is in reply to something Clough has written in answer to Arnold's talk of artistry in Letter 7.

(For Arnold's elaborate criticism of Burns, see 'The Study of Poetry', *Essays in Criticism*, 2nd series, 43–53.)

⁴ 'My man' in this, and Letters 14 and 15, is obviously Lord Lansdowne; 'The vulgar fussy Yankee Minister at Paris' is Richard Rush, American Ambassador, who, on February 28, made an address to the new Government at the Hôtel de Ville. Finding himself, as he said, at too great a distance to await instructions from Washington, he took the liberty of congratulating the new régime. He pointed out his joy that American principles of government were now to have trial in France, quoted from George Washington, and made a profound impression on the French people who were delighted by this formal recognition of their republic. (Described in *Times* of February 29, p. 6, and late edition of March 1; for recapitulation, see *Times*, Thursday, March 2, p. 5.)

⁵ The reference is interesting, in view of the little Arnold ever says of Fielding or of the novel in general.

⁶ The *Bhagavad Gita*. (See Letter 9.)

9

[March 4 seems the reasonable date for this letter, because Clough has apparently, in his answer to the immediately preceding letter of March 1, touched upon the Oriental poem and the address of Ambassador Rush at Paris.

The question about publication doubtless concerns Clough's projected book of poems with his friend, Thomas Burbidge. See introductory note to letter No. 4.]

[London] Saturday [March 4, 1848]

Dear Clough

I did not at first answer your question because I wanted to consider a little: which I do best as I walk past the shops in the street: I think the double columned large 8ᵛᵒ advantageous in itself—but it does not do so well for a first publication as it seems to imply a large sale and among the people. I think therefore you are almost forced by the decencies to begin in the 12ᵐᵒ.

It seems as if the French Government¹ might fall into the relaxation naturally consequent on great tension and trust to routine like other people: in which case they will infallibly be done for: nothing but a perennial enthusiasm can now work France—which may or may not be impossible. They cannot be Americans thank God if they would.

If you do not see the difference between Rush's step and that of his bated imitators[2] I quit the subject.

The Indians distinguish between meditation or absorption—and knowledge: and between abandoning practice, and abandoning the fruits of action and all respect thereto. This last is a supreme step, and dilated on throughout the Poem.[3]

A man sits waiting for me   Goodbye

M. ARNOLD.—

[1] The Provisional Government was in an *embarras* about a mode of conducting the elections to name permanent officers of the Republic. It was not, indeed, until the night of Arnold's letter, if one takes March 4 as the date, that the Government finally fixed the convocation of the Electoral Assemblies for April 9, and the meeting of the Constitutional Assembly for April 20. Meanwhile, the excitement at Paris had considerably calmed down, the official dispatches reporting it as 'perfectly tranquil'. (*Times*, March 4, p. 5.)

[2] Most of the other important ambassadors at Paris, although they expressed confidence in the new government of France, did not, like Mr. Rush, convey formal recognition. On March 2 *The Times* (pp. 5 and 6) had told of the second visit to Lamartine from Lord Normanby, the British minister at Paris, who assured him of the friendly disposition of the British Government, but made it clear that this was as far as the Government could go at the time. *The Times* of March 4 (p. 5) recounted Lord Normanby's official communication of dispatches from Lord Palmerston. 'Lord Palmerston announced to Lord Normanby . . . that if diplomatic usage does not authorize the English government to accredit definitive diplomatic agents to the Provisional Government, the moment the Provisional Government shall have been converted into a definitive Government by the National Assembly, the English Government will accredit its Ambassador to the French Republic. In the mean time Lord Palmerston authorizes Lord Normanby to maintain with the Provisional Government of the Republic not only the usual intercourse, but all the relations of good understanding and amity which ought to animate the two Governments.'

[3] These comments clearly reveal that the poem, also mentioned in Letters 8 and 10, is the *Bhagavad Gita*. Much of it, I am inclined to think, heavily influenced Arnold's own *Resignation* and other early poems.

10

[The two letters that follow may be dated by their contents. All the European countries were nervous about possible aggression from the new Provisional Government of France.

Lamartine, as Minister of Foreign Affairs, addressed on
March 2 a manifesto to the diplomatic agents of France
throughout Europe. On the whole, it was very reassuring,
and asserted a desire for peace and the general safety of
Europe. It did, however, deny the existence of the Treaty
of 1815, and expressed its warm faith that republican principles
should increase, though by no active propaganda, throughout
Europe. The manifesto was printed in the *Moniteur* of March 5
and recopied by the late editions of *The Times* the next day.
See reprint in *Times*, March 7, p. 5.]

L.[ansdowne] House Monday [March 6, 1848]
My dear Clough
You must come this week if you come but on my conscience I do not think it is worth while. The squalor of the
place, the faint earthy orange smell, the dimness of the
light, the ghostly ineffectualness of the sub-actors, the self-
consciousness of Fanny Kemble, the harshness of Macready,
the unconquerable difficulty of the play, altogether gave
me sensations of wretchedness during the performance of
Othello the other night I am sure you would have shared
with me had you been there.[1] I go no more, except to
accompany you. But what are your plans about coming
to town, any way?

You have seen Lamartine's circular. The Austrian and
English aristocracies to whom it comes the latter particularly will simply not understand it. Vague theorizing out
of his 'Girondins' they will say here.[2] Yet no more will the
people here than their rulers. Therefore while I own that
the riding class here are incapable of distilling the oil you
speak of, let us add that the people would be at any rate
insensible to it. It is this—this *wide and deepspread intelligence*
that makes the French seem to themselves in the van of
Europe.[3] People compare a class here with a class there
the best in each, and then wonder at Michelet's or Guizot's
vanity. I don't think you have done them justice in this
respect. Do you remember your pooh-poohing the revue
des deux Mondes, and my expostulating that the final expression up to the present time of European opinion, without fantastic individual admixture, was *current* there: not
emergent here and there in a great writer,—but the *atmo-*

sphere of the commonplace man as well as of the Genius. This is the secret of their power: our weakness is that in an age where all tends to the triumph of the logical absolute reason we neither courageously have thrown ourselves into this movement like the French: nor yet have driven our feet into the solid ground of our individuality as spiritual, poetic, profound *persons*. Instead of this we have stood *up* hesitating: seeming to refuse the first line on the ground that the second is our *natural* one—yet not taking this. How long halt ye between two opinions: woe to the modern nation, which will neither be philosophe nor philosopher. Eh?

Yours with apologies for longness
M. ARNOLD.

Yet it is something for a nation to feel that the only true line is its natural one?

¹ On February 21, William Charles Macready and Fanny Kemble Butler had begun an engagement of eight Shakespearian plays at the Princess's Theatre. The performance of *Othello* that Arnold saw was doubtless that of February 25. Macready had written in his Diary after the rehearsal of the night before that Mrs. Butler's 'many affectations prevent *her* from *being Desdemona*'. His first rehearsal with her had made him record, 'I have never seen any one so bad, so unnatural, so affected, so conceited. . . . I must strive, and be careful, and hope in God for myself'. However much he would have joined Arnold's verdict upon Fanny Kemble, Macready would have differed upon the estimate of his own performance. He has: 'February 25th—Acted Othello with all the strength I had, and, I think, *well*.' (*The Diaries of William Charles Macready*, edited by William Toynbee, Chapman & Hall, London, 1912, ii. 385-6.) The theatrical critic of *The Examiner*, for February 26, praised Macready, but wished Mrs. Butler's work were more her own and less that of a school (p. 133).

² This prediction was justified by the highly sceptical leading article *The Times* devoted the next morning to the manifesto (edition of Tuesday, March 7, p. 4). Lamartine's *Histoire des Girondins*, published first periodically and then entire in 1848, was considered by many one of the leading causes of the new revolution.

³ See the letter to his sister four days later: 'What agitates me is this, if the new state of things succeeds in France, social changes are *inevitable* here and elsewhere, for no one looks on seeing his neighbour mending without asking himself if he cannot mend in the same way; but, without waiting for the result, the spectacle of France is likely to breed great agitation here, and such is the state of our masses that their movements now *can* only be brutal plundering and destroying.

73

And if they wait, there is no one, as far as one sees, to train them to conquer, by their attitude and superior conviction; the deep ignorance of the middle and upper classes, and their feebleness of vision becoming, if possible, daily more apparent. You must by this time begin to see what people mean by placing France *politically* in the van of Europe; it is the *intelligence* of their *idea-moved masses* which makes them, politically, as far superior to the *insensible masses* of England as to the Russian serfs, and at the same time they do not threaten the educated world with the intolerable *laideur* of the well-fed American masses, so deeply anti-pathetic to continental Europe.' (*Letters*, i. 6.)

I I

L[ansdowne] House. Ash Wednesday.
[March 8, 1848]

Dear Clough

Come this week if possible for as the season advances I keep hoping to get away to Oxford myself if possible. You cannot be sure beforehand of what you will see. Macbeth is the best—or Wolsey.[1]

I have been a constant attender on the emeutes here—endeavouring to impress on the mob that not royalty but aristocracy—primogeniture—large land and mill owners were their true enemies here. But they draw it very mild at present.[2]

By trivialities do you mean novels as opposed to Comte and them of that kidney—Figaro as opposed to the Contrat Social. For amongst a *people* of readers the litterature is a greater engine than the philosophy. Which last they change very fast—oh said a F[renc]hman to me the other day—Comte—Comte has been quite passé these 10 years.

Besides in the Revue[3] one has the *applied* ideas on all points:—of litterature, of politics—Polish—Irish—Italian. The value of the F[renc]h movement being always not absolute but relative I prefer to read their relative not their absolute litterature. Which last is tiresome what I have seen of it. Seditious songs have nourished the F[renc]h people much more than the Socialist: philosophers: though they may formulize their wants through the mouths of these.

—Well but come—

The Prov[isional] Gov[ernment] is said to be divided —Garnier Pages Cremieux and Marie versus Ledru Rollin,

Flocon, and Louis Blanc. Lamartine neutral—inclining to the first set. Not a bad electoral scheme, as they are?

The Examiner article[4] is by Carlyle—and how solemn, how deeply *restful* it strikes on one amidst the heat and vain words that are everywhere just now—Yet the thoughts extracted and abstractedly stated, are every newspaper's: it is the style and feeling by which the beloved man appears. Apply this, Infidel, to the Oriental Poem.[5] How short could Mill write Job?

Carlyle says, I am told—'The human race, has now arrived at the last stage of Jack assification.'

Yours

M. ARNOLD.

[1] See first paragraph of preceding letter. Macready's first week at the Princess's Theatre had included *Macbeth*, *Othello*, and *Henry the Eighth* with Macready as Wolsey.

[2] Monday, March 6, and Tuesday, March 7, had seen rather exciting riots in Trafalgar Square, which grew out of an open-air meeting on the Income Tax, attended by few, indeed, whom the tax could possibly concern. (See Arnold's *Letters*, p. 4.)

[3] The tribute that Arnold here pays the *Revue des Deux Mondes* is one of his sincerest convictions. In *The Function of Criticism* he praises it as an organ 'having for its main function to understand and utter the best that is known and thought in the world, existing, it may be said, as just an organ for a free play of the mind', the like of which does not exist in England. (*Essays in Criticism*, 1st series, p. 19.)

[4] The article on Louis Philippe appeared in the *Examiner* of March 4, 1848, pp. 145–6. Arnold wrote to his mother concerning it: 'I send you the Examiner with an article of Carlyle's. How deeply restful it comes upon one, amidst the hot dizzy trash one reads about these changes everywhere. . . . The source of repose in Carlyle's article is that he alone puts aside the din and whirl and brutality which envelop a movement of the masses, to fix his thoughts on its ideal invisible character.' (*Letters*, p. 4.)

[5] The *Bhagavad Gita*, mentioned in the two preceding letters, and apparently appreciated more by Arnold than by Clough. The heightening by which the poem attains distinction is akin to that which Carlyle gains. The Book of Job could be reduced to a logical skeleton by John Stuart Mill, whereby it would lose its power and charm.

12

[Clough's MS. journal shows that he was in London with Arnold on Saturday and Sunday, March 18 and 19. The contemplated attendance upon Macready apparently gave way to Miss

Fortescue's performance of *Sweethearts and Wives* at the Haymarket Theatre. Clough returned to Oriel on Monday, March 20.

During that visit the two friends doubtless discussed Clough's intention of resigning his fellowship, on the ground that his inability to accept some of the Thirty-nine Articles made his position at Oriel untenable. See his letter of February 20 in answer to Shairp's protest against his resigning, *Prose Remains*, p. 121. His tutorship he was already relinquishing in April. Arnold in the present letter is apparently discussing a draft of formal resignation, and expresses his conviction that revolt within the colleges against the Articles will encourage those who might like to see Oxford dissociated from them.

The letter may also be dated by its contents. See notes at end.]

[London] Friday. [March 24?, 1848]

Dear Clough

Receipt takes a p.

I would not say *unworthily*—for that sounds like conscious peculation.

And perhaps the second Paragraph is a little obscure and heavy. But the general thing is right, I think—though I would have had it shorter. Quite right to wait about signing it. I care very little about it—except that it is one of the few changes I think *clearly desirable* as well as *necessary*.

And to know that there are traitors within the place mightily enheartens the attaquers.

Tell me when you have fixed on your line, and I will write to Stanley.

—I hear Cobden's slip about the American Consul has done him great harm: the House firmly believing he told a lie.[1] I cannot say how it was with him: but by Yorkshire and Lancashire eo perventum est that such a feat in their champion would not much shock them.

—A friend of Morris's[2] says—now is the time to preach Christ to France—Germany cannot do it, England must.— I like the king of Prussia, but he is misdated and misplaced, I fear, even in Germany.[3]

—I was glad to see you the other day, and spiritually to shake hands. Do not let us forsake one another: we have the common quality, now rare, of being unambitious, I think. Some must be contented not to be at the top.

I have G. Sand's letter—do you want it? I do not like it so well as at first. For my soul I cannot *understand* this violent praise of the people. I praise a fagot where-of the several twigs are nought: but a *people?* ⁴

yours

M. ARNOLD.

¹ For complete details of Richard Cobden's difficulty in the House of Commons on March 20, 1848, see Appendix IV, p. 170–1.

² The name was fairly common at Oxford during Arnold's time there. The reference here is probably to John Brande Morris, of Balliol, and later fellow at Exeter, 1837–46. He was Hebrew lecturer, and finally seceded to Rome. The other likely person is William (O'Connor) Morris, who was at Oriel during the same time. (Foster, *Alumni Oxon.* (1715–1886), pp. 987–8.)

³ The French Revolution fast spread its influence over all Europe. In Berlin serious riots occurred on March 18–19. During these days and consequently, King Friedrich Wilhelm IV had shown commendable wisdom and courage. Already having granted some popular concessions, he appealed to Berliners to return to peace and order, asking them to heed the paternal voice of their king, and look to the great German union which Prussia was to effect before long. *The Times*, of the very day of Arnold's letter, praised the King's policy and his spirit, and printed a dispatch from Berlin which said, 'Thousands and thousands thronged on the afternoon of Monday towards the Palace, and with one voice, all at once began to sing the German Te Deum, "Now let us all praise God". The bodies of the fallen were carried to the churches in solemn silence, under the intonation of the celebrated popular hymn, "Jesus, my Redeemer, liveth," the King, bareheaded, like every one else, seeing them pass from the balcony.' (*Times*, Friday, March 24, 1848, p. 5.) It will also be recalled that Arnold had been given sympathetic ideas of the Prussian king by his friend Chevalier Bunsen, the Prussian ambassador at London from 1845 to 1854.

⁴ See George Sand's two *Lettres au peuple* of March 7 and 19, 1848. *Questions politiques et sociales*, Calmann Lévy, Paris, 1879, pp. 202–24.

13

[This letter is obviously linked to the foregoing by the repeated reference to Cobden's embarrassment in the House of Commons, and by the reference to George Sand's letter promised Clough in the last.

The disturbances of 1848 inflamed with a new zeal the Young Ireland party, former followers of O'Connell, but now under more radical leadership of Smith O'Brien and Thomas Francis

Meagher, who gradually threatened open rebellion. *The Times* was the ardent supporter of Lord Clarendon, who, since his appointment in May of the previous year, had been generally admired for his tact and wisdom, and especially for his efforts to instruct the Irish people in better methods of farming. Strenuous in its demand for further coercive measures in Ireland, it laid bare the full gravity of the growing rebellion on Wednesday, March 29, and defended Clarendon's determination to crush any sedition. On Friday, March 31, a long editorial gave Clarendon most lavish praise. The issue of April 4 recounted the glowing tribute paid to Clarendon in Parliament by Lord Jocelyn, who asked Lord John Russell if the time had not come at last for stern measures against the Irish rebels. On Friday, April 7, Earl Grey finally introduced his bill for the 'better security of the crown' in Ireland. See p. 4 in each of the issues mentioned.

Arnold's attitude toward the Irish question predicts his later essays on that subject.]

[London, early April 1848]

Dear Clough

I had used the same words almost to Blackett about Cobden and the H.[ouse] of C.[ommons]

—And the newspapers—my God!—But they and the H.[ouse] of C.[ommons] represent England at the present moment very fairly.

I cannot believe that the mass of people here would see much bloodshed in Ireland without asking themselves what they were shedding it to *uphold*. And when the answer came —1. a chimerical Theory about some possible dangerous foreign alliances with independent Ireland: 2. a body of Saxon landlords—3. a Saxon Ch.[urch] Estab[lishmen]t their consciences must smite them. I think I told you that the performance of Polyeucte[1] suggested to me the right of large bodies of men to have what article they liked produced for them. The Irish article is not to my taste: still we have no really superiour article to offer them, which alone can justify the violence offered by a Lycurgus or a Cromwell to a foolish nation, as unto Children.—It makes me sick to hear Ld. Clarendon praised so: as if he was doing anything but cleverly managing the details of an imposture.

—I do not want England to attack Russia:[2] she has no real share in this movement: and there is no good in her having an apparent one.

Expectandum est.—I send G. S.

yours
M. A.

[1] Arnold had seen Corneille's play in Paris.

[2] For details of the somewhat specially centred, but none the less definite agitation in England against Russia, see Appendix IV, p. 171–2.

14

[On March 30, Ralph Waldo Emerson visited Oxford, where he formed a strong attachment for Clough, who acted as his guide and host. The two week-ends following, Clough went to London, where he was again with Emerson, and also with Arnold. Clough MS. journal.

On Monday, April 10, the day he returned to Oriel, occurred the famous Chartist demonstration, which Feargus O'Connor had arranged for Kennington Common. The Duke of Wellington had supervised elaborate defensive preparations, with the result that Arnold, after his talk with Lord Lansdowne ('my man'), here describes.]

[London] 4¾ Monday. [April 10, 1848]

Dear Clough

I am not sure of having time to send you a paper: I am only just come from my man—but all is perfectly quiet— The Chartists gave up at once in the greatest fright at seeing the preparations: braggarts as they are, says my man: and Fergus O'Connor and Co—after giving themselves into custody expressed the greatest thankfulness to the Government that their polite offer was not taken advantage of on condition of their making the crowd disperse.—Then came ½ an hour after, the hard rain.

The petition is quietly progressing in cabs, unattended, to Westminster.

—There may be a little row in the evening, from the congregated pickpockets etc.—but nothing much I think certainly.

Yours
M. A.

15

[This letter can be assigned to the very day by the events it
describes. In order to observe the scenes of the late revolution,
Clough went to Paris for the month of May. There he was
almost daily with Emerson. The Paris mob had already begun
to embarrass the Government. Sunday, May 15, had seen
that memorable rioting in the streets, when the mob, with
whom Lamartine's influence had declined greatly, believing
the government's promise to secure employment had been
broken, invaded the Assembly and attempted a counter-
revolution. In a remarkable letter to Stanley written from Paris
on May 19, Clough had burlesqued Carlyle's style in writing
French history, beginning, 'Ichabod, Ichabod, the glory is
departed!' See full text in Clough's *Prose Remains*, pp. 127, 128.

The parliamentary journal of *The Times* for Wednesday,
May 24, tells of the events of the night before in the House,
which Arnold relays from London. For details see notes at
end of letter.]

Dear Clough   London. Wednesday. [May 24, 1848]
    Thanks for all favours.

    I broke my anti-journal rule to see what was become of
Hume's Motion this morning, and find it put off—with a
stinging speech from Cobden at O'Connor—an unfortunate declaration (I think) from Lord John which Hume
turns to account in his address to the people and perhaps
more remarkable than any, a speech from Milner Gibson,
who has got quite clear now.[1]

    What you say about France is just about the impression
I get from the accounts of things there—it must be dis-
heartening to the believers in progress—or at least in any
progress but progress en ligne spirale which Goethe allows
man[2]—tho: from him I scarcely understand this concession.
If you remember it is exactly Wordsworth's account of the
matter in his letter in the 'friend'[3]—wch is curious—but
this you don't much want to hear.

    —There was a report here the other day that George Sand[4]
was arrested—not true I suppose—but how charming the
beginning of F.[rancois] le Champi is and how did you
like Teverino—Her true style now, indeed?—Milnes[5] perhaps you find very pleasant alone or where there is no

necessity for him briller: it is that fatal need which unsexes quite the sweetest-natured perhaps who are not at the same time philosophers.

A sudden thought strikes me—is my man going to the Derby[6]—for at the door stands a brougham with a postillion and pair. . . .

I met Martin the American Chargé d'affaires to Rome[7] the other day—such a contrast—so exuberant jolly and all-permitting—praying for the stability of this country, looking on the American revolution as a mere political developement against the will of a Tory govt.: and being, not a triumph over the England nation—and equally disliking and despising the Yankees. From the south therefore—a strong head and face, and truly genial—he only said, Sir and Ma'am that was wrong—alas, the Children of this world etc.—

Last night I met R. Palmer[8] who worded me like the Devil. however I praised him for his votes and attitude in Parliament. Have you seen an article in the Examiner signed M. in answer to Carlyle on Ireland. Mill's, they say.[9] —Mithridate was a young man's effort[10]—but you know you are a mere d—d depth hunter in poetry and therefore exclusive furiously. You might write a speech in Phèdre— Phedra loquitur—but you could not write Phèdre. And when you adopt this or that form you must sacrifice much to the ensemble, and that form in return for admirable effects demands immense sacrifices and precisely in that quarter where your nature will not allow you to make them. Have you read Andromaque, and what do you think of Rachel— greater in what she is than in her creativity, eh? exactly the converse of Jenny Lind.[11] By the way what an enormous obverse that young woman and excellent singer has.

Farewell—Farewell—your judgement cannot allow you to get the common slow picture of Beethoven. I have got a good Goethe—the og.German—quite by accident.

M. A.

I've a great mind to send you Bohn's Catalogue with this by post and not to affranchir.

[1] Joseph Hume's motion for extending the electoral franchise was put off at 11.15 p.m. until June 20. O'Connor, the Chartist leader,

claimed that this postponement was only added evidence of the attempt of the middle classes further to trifle with the working men. Cobden, in turn, severely rebuked O'Connor for setting the masses always against any movement that could really help them. Lord John Russell, in course of the debate, said he believed the middle and working classes generally wanted neither the Charter nor Hume's reforms. On the principal page of *The Times* next morning, Hume called attention to Lord John's remark and asked his supporters now to let there be no doubt as to their convictions (*Times*, May 24, 1848, pp. 2–4). Milner Gibson's speech was a strong protest against the way the House could trifle time on empty matters, and a sharp reply to George Bentinck's attack upon free trade.

² 'The circle that humanity must complete is clear enough, and in spite of vast pauses which barbarism has made, has already more than once run through its course. If one cares to ascribe to it a spiral movement, then it returns continually to that region through which it has once before passed. In this way all true opinions and all errors are repeated.' (Goethe, 'Geschichte der Farbenlehre', *Sämtliche Werke*, Jubiläums-Ausgabe, xl. 120.)

³ And Wordsworth has it: 'The progress of the species neither is nor can be like that of a Roman road in a right line. It may be more justly compared to that of a river . . . etc. etc.' (See *The Complete Works of Samuel Taylor Coleridge*, New York, 1853, ii. 362.)

⁴ George Sand's newspaper, *La Vraie République*, had disapproved of the new government, which it held was allowing the provinces to be controlled by the people of Paris. The rumour of her arrest was reported in *The Times* of Monday, May 22 (p. 6). She did retire to the country towards the end of May. (See Clough's *Prose Remains*, p. 131.)

⁵ Richard Monckton Milnes, Lord Houghton (1809–85), author and statesman, was Clough's companion during part of the Paris visit. He was then in Parliament. For Arnold's more flattering estimate of him, see *Letters*, i. 116–17.

⁶ The Derby which Lord Lansdowne ('my man') may have been contemplating was run at Epsom Downs on Wednesday, May 24 (*Times*, May 25, p. 5).

⁷ Mr. Jacob L. Martin, Chargé d'Affaires at Paris from October 1, 1846, to June 28, 1847, was given similar appointment to the Papal States in April 1848. He was in England during the spring of 1848 for his health. He left England for Rome on July 17, 1848, dying little more than a month later from apoplexy. (Record furnished by courtesy of the Department of State, Washington.)

⁸ Roundell Palmer, whom Arnold and Clough knew at Oxford, had been made Conservative member for Plymouth in the elections of 1847.

⁹ Mill's answer to Carlyle was contained in the *Examiner* for May 13, 1848, pp. 307–8.

¹⁰ During his sojourn in Paris, Clough saw Racine's *Mithridate* on Thursday, May 18, and *Phèdre* on Tuesday, May 9 (MS. journal). Arnold's regard for Rachel is commemorated in his sonnets to her and

in his prose confession of how in his youth, after a first sight of her at the Edinburgh Theatre, in the part of Hermione, he followed her to Paris, where for two months he never missed one of her representations. (See his *The French Play in London*.) In that same essay Arnold expressed his faith in Rachel's immense intellectual superiority over the later Sarah Bernhardt. On May 11 Clough had written to his sister that he had been 'a little disappointed' with Rachel's Phèdre, but that he was going again to study the play.

¹¹ Jenny Lind, the toast of London, was again singing at Her Majesty's Theatre. The next evening after Arnold's letter (May 25) she was to reach the high point of her season in her first appearance in *Lucia di Lammermoor*.

16

[Clough returned from Paris to London on Tuesday, June 6 (MS. Journal), and found himself, as he wrote to Stanley, 'safe again under the umbrageous blessing of constitutional monarchy, at Long's Hotel, Bond Street'. He remained a few days with his friends, heard Emerson in three lectures, and returned to Oxford on Saturday. The following Tuesday, June 13, he was back in London, his diary for the next day recording, 'Carlyle with Mat'. He made another London excursion the same month, finally going by way of short visits at Rugby and Lichfield, to his home in Liverpool, which he reached on July 8 (MS. Journal). On July 15, he saw Emerson sail for America, his journal for that day recording, 'Explicit liber Emersonianus'.

Shortly afterward, in his journal, Clough records these significant reflections:

'To some special want or weakness some special help may respond—a look of a friend, a sight of a great Man, a passage of a book may relieve this or that distemper—the presence of her voice or his eye—Emerson's talk, the discourse of Carlyle, a sermon from Arnold may dissipate this disease, heal this sore, is specific for one or another. But a Presence I acknowledge, I am conscious of a Power, whose name is Panacea— whose visits indeed are seldom and I know not where to bespeak them; but who itself is Prescription and Recovery; and of whom though invisible I feel it is about my path and about my bed and spieth out all my ways. And in such feeling will I if need be endure, and be without stoicism more than stoical.' (Clough MSS.)

Arnold is troubled about what Clough will do after leaving Oriel. The deep concern of this letter and of those immediately following contrasts strikingly with Clough's earlier worries over the young Balliol scholar who preferred to fish rather than to prepare for his examinations.

The date of the letter is postulated by the events it describes.]

London. Thursday.
[late June or early July 1848]

Dear Clough

Do you know that Ld. Lovelace's son's tutorship is again open?

Or do you indeed as you suggested mean to become one of those 'misanthropical hermits who are incapable of seeing that the Muse willingly *accompanies* life but that in no wise does she understand to *guide* it'?[1]

I spare you the rest about 'nimbly recovering oneself' etc. of which you will guess the to you quite alien author.

—I am divided between a desire to see those cursed poltroons the Lombards well kicked[2]—and to have so ugly a race as the Germans removed from Italy. I suppose for travellers it is desirable that the Germans should remain as police and the useful arts generally are unknown to the Italians.

What a nice state of things in France. The New Gospel is adjourned for this bout. If one had ever hoped any thing from such a set of d——d grimacing liars as their prophets one would be very sick just now.[3] I returned and saw under the sun etc.—but time and chance happeneth unto all.

—If you mean to do nothing why not emigrate? Shake yourself—it is easier to discover what we *can* do than our vanity lets us think. For God's sake don't mope, for from that no good can come.

I have not even begun the work you allude to in your last. your friend—

M. A.

---

[1] This quotation has not been identified. It may well be that Arnold is preaching humorously from an imaginary work of his own; that he, in other words, is himself the 'alien author'.

[2] *The Times* of July 7, and of the day following also, gave news of the refusal of the Lombard Provisional Government at Milan to accept Austria's offer of independence on condition the Lombards shouldered part of the national debt. The revolt against Austria had

been going on since the first of the year, the actual war beginning on March 17. Arnold had probably been struck by the way the Lombards showed their hatred of Austria. Great ladies shunned the Scala because it was a royal theatre; and the young ones refused to dance with Austrian officers. The lotteries, with their potential state revenue, were ignored; Austrian families were cut socially; and the Lombards had nationally given up smoking to prevent an Austrian profit from the tobacco tax. From this last boycott many amusing reports had been furnished the English journals. (For Arnold's more formal analysis of the German type, see *On the Study of Celtic Literature*, p. 74 ff., and 'Amiel', *Essays in Criticism*, 2nd series, pp. 323–4.)

³ This is doubtless Arnold's feeling about the period following the four days of June 23–7 at Paris (for details, see Appendix IV, pp. 172–3), when an insurrection occurred that marked certainly the final hour for those men who had risen to power in February.

17

[Clough has evidently made some protest against what Arnold wrote in the preceding letter about the necessity of finding employment.

The continued abuse of the Lombards also shows the relationship between the two letters and fixes the date of this one.]

[London] Lundi. [July 1848]

Dear Clough

Did I ever say to you a fragment—

'this little which we are
Swims on an obscure much we might have been'

I do not say I discern the *right* way for you: have we one? but such a way as the βουλή and νόος* of man can shape out, pace Fato, that I tried to discern. This β and ν do not talk of *the* absolutely right but of *a* promising method with ourselves. If you do nothing I see some dangers for you. and I suggest what precaution prudence suggests. But I dare say you will not be satisfied till you have tried your own way: if you think you have any absolute one I am sure you will not. follow it therefore—you remember ὁ μὴ δαρεὶς ἄνθρωπος οὐ παιδεύεται.† Tell me what you are

* 'will (reason)' and 'perceptive intelligence'.

† 'The man who has not been thrashed is not disciplined'. A common Greek proverb.

doing—and do not suppose I make pretension to *know* you
or anybody.
    When do you publish? do you go on writing? You see
your review journal. Those Lombard republicans are
s—s, if ever such there were.

Yours,
M. A.

would I were hence,

———————————

18

London, July 20 [1848]

My dear Clough
    Goethe says somewhere[1] that the Zeitgeist when he was
young caused everyone to adopt the Wolfian theories about
Homer, himself included: and that when he was in middle
age the same Zeitgeist caused them to leave these theories
for the hypothesis of one poem and one author: inferring
that in these matters there is no certainty, but alternating
dispositions. This view, as congenial to me as uncongenial,
I suspect, to you, causes me, while I confess that productions like your Adam and Eve[2] are not suited to me at
present, yet to feel no confidence that they may not be
quite right and calculated to suit others. The good feature
in all your poems is the sincerity that is evident in them:
which always produces a powerful effect on the reader—
and which most people with the best intentions lose totally
when they sit down to write. The spectacle of a writer
striving evidently to get breast to breast with reality is
always full of instruction and very invigorating—and here
I always feel you have the advantage of me: 'much may be
seen, tho: nothing can be solved'—weighs upon me in
writing. However it must be continued to tread the wine
press alone.
    Ewald[3] has just published a final volume: Stanley[3] says
he is not at all offensive like Newman,[4] looking on Judaism
as a religion: but that poor Newman being insane should
not be judged harshly. Ewald judges the new revolutions
very harshly tho:—and rates the Germans soundly for their

imitations of the French—that shallow and Godless people, he says.

I have told Stanley of your intention to resign your fellowship—and Walrond: and I think Blackett—but no one else, and shall I think have strength given me to let it go no further. But we are not in our own hands and can only watch and pray.

God bless you: there is a God, but he is not well-conceived of by all.

Yrs. affct.

M. ARNOLD.

¹ See Goethe, *Schriften zur Literatur*, 3rd part, section entitled: 'Homer noch einmal (1827)', in his *Sämtliche Werke*, Jubiläums-Ausgabe, xxxviii, pp. 77–8.

² The imperfect manuscript of 'Adam and Eve' is published in Clough's collected poems under title of *Fragments of the Mystery of the Fall*.

³ Arthur Stanley had made the acquaintance of Georg Heinrich August von Ewald (1803–75), the German scholar and theologian, whose study of the Hebrew origins was attracting wide interest. Stanley had met him on the Continent during a holiday.

⁴ For Francis Newman, see p. 115, note 3.

19

[This letter clearly follows on the one before it by its consideration of Clough's resigning his fellowship and of the poem about Adam and Eve.]

London. Thursday. [July–early August 1848]
Dear Clough

I had lost your note and was purposing to send all your papers to Liverpool—but I have found it again and send them to the address you desired.

I have done you no harm by telling—I have told no one else: Stanley inferred you were certainly *going* to have told him: no doubt said I. Redcar, Yorkshire my family are at ¹ —but to Fox How with a 'to be forwarded' would have found them thoughtless villain.

—I meant to say that your treatment of Adam and Eve's story rather offended me: but then I was quite in another way just now

The Gregs[2] are just the thing for you as a family—without pretension, intelligent etc. 150 £ is little certainly, but it means living in the house I conclude. But I should make plug[3] represent to them that a real graduated experienced well-known Oxford top-sawyer would snuff disdainfully *in his opinion* at such a price: they must have been thinking of some inferior dissenting-made article. But if they excused their poverty (as they are embarrassed just now) I should say the family and the Lake Country made up for an extra £50. You have £50 a year of your own at least—and God knows you have few expenses as to dress etc. Still I should use jackall plug to some extent to feel and smell about. What do you want to write to my people about.

Yours ever
M. A.

[1] On August 12, Edward Quillinan, neighbour of the Arnolds in the Lake Country, wrote to Henry Crabb Robinson, 'The Arnolds, pleased with Redcar, continue there till next month.' (*Correspondence of Henry Crabb Robinson with the Wordsworth Circle*, ii. 676.)

[2] William Rathbone Greg (1809–81) lived in the Lake Country at this time. He was suffering financial reverses that, by 1850, were to make him give up his business altogether. Clough's journal for August 15, reads, 'chez Greg'.

[3] The 'jackall plug' of the letter is Charles Thomas Arnold, master at Rugby (see p. 57, note 1). June 28, according to the records in his diary, Clough stopped at Rugby for a time, 'chez C. T. A.'

20

[Lord Lovelace (William King) was requiring a tutor for his second son, by his first wife Ada, the daughter of Lord Byron. Arnold advises Clough to consider this opportunity at Esher, together with that at Mr. Greg's. See preceding letter.]

London. Ag. 12, [18]48.

My dear Love

'By our own spirits etc etc.' [1]

I desire you should have some occupation—I think it desirable for everyone—very much so for you. Besides since the Baconian era wisdom is not found in desarts: and you again especially need the world and yet will not be absorbed by any quantity of it.—That Greg's £150 is monstrous: probably the natural history is no more than would be most beneficial for you to learn and most health-ful—you poor subjective, you—do you not care to know quo sidere etc. But a person like you might probably soon turn the education your own way. And Esher is a heaven upon earth for beauty.

—I have been thinking about you for the Co-Examiner-ship with Lingen: it is the mathematical one—Temple[2] says it would take you from 6 to 7 hours p^r diem from now at mathematics to be up to the mark by Xmas when the appointment is made.—Eh? Altogether I don't think you'd stand that—and when you have begun the work is very hard—it is possible too Lingen might wish a less extra-ordinary colleague: but efforts might be made if you liked: £500 a year, and no oaths.—But, considering Esher and all other things, I am for L^d. King. Why did you not tell me or some one who might have remonstrated before you answered Stanley in the negative, who weeps and answers not. He is in Scotland—knowest thou where? I know not. —What are you doing—reading? writing?

M. A.

[1] 'By our own spirits are we deified—.' (Wordsworth, *Resolution and Independence*, l. 47.)
[2] Frederick Temple (1821–1902), the old Oxford friend of Clough and Arnold, and later Archbishop of Canterbury. He and others had suggested the Education Office, where Ralph Lingen had gone in 1847. (For Lingen, see p. 143, note 4.) Stanley, hearing of Clough's having resigned his fellowship, has also apparently offered assistance.

21

L.[ansdowne] H.[ouse]. Friday
[August or early September 1848]

Dear Clough

The exercise of the intellect is to you not grievous but pleasant: therefore I send you Edward's[1] questions which I am incapable of fitly answering, and which if you will solve and send to Redcar to him it were well. I know you can do this without book—so wonderful a thing is practice.

I have been reading with equal surprize and profit lately the short work—

> 'Of that lame slave who in Nicopolis
> Taught Arrian, when Vespasian's brutal son
> Cleared Rome of what most sham'd him— [2]

There's for you but this style is not hard tho: rather taking. What dispute is now going on

> 'Where young Archestes doth with Ister join,
> Ister, Tethys and Ocean's sixth-born son.' [3]

—But the difference between Herodotus and Sophocles is that the former sought over all the world's surface for that interest the latter found within man. [4]

Yours affectionately
M. ARNOLD.

[1] Edward Penrose Arnold, one of Matthew's younger brothers, was studying at Redcar (see preceding letter) for his examinations at Oxford.

[2] The first draft of the tribute to Epictetus contained in Arnold's early sonnet, *To a Friend*. The 'short work' is the *Enchiridion*.

[3] The second quotation is probably also something Arnold himself has written. Ister, in Hesiod and Sophocles, and generally in classical literature, is the name of the present Danube. A long search, with the help of several classical scholars, has failed, however, to find the word 'Archestes'. Apparently it refers to some tributary of the Danube, perhaps the Arges, a considerable stream west of Bucharest. About 130 kilometres to the west of the same city is the little village of Arcesti. There is, of course, the Artanes, which flows into the Danube from Thrace and which is mentioned by Herodotus. Arnold is doubtless thinking of the trouble in the Danube valley that marked the general European crises of 1848. I should welcome any clue about 'Archestes' and its associations.

[4] The reference to Herodotus and Sophocles has little to do with the fragment above it. Having named a contemporary event, Arnold is struck immediately with the vanity of such interests. They are shows of the world that pass away; for example, see how clearly he states this idea in Letter 32. The historian's survey of *all* action is less revealing than the tragic writer's insight into a single individual.

<hr>

22

[It is a significant fact that each of Clough's three principal poems was inspired by vacations. The *Bothie* was one of these, and it was composed during the month after his return from

the Lake Country, where he visited during late August and
the first few days of September. The pastoral was directly
prompted by a reading of Longfellow's *Evangeline*. The chief
pleasure Clough derived from its publication was that of
watching the amazement of serious gentlemen who expected
him to write an apologia for his resigning at Oriel.

Meanwhile, Clough at home in Liverpool, Arnold had
escaped to the Continent for a rest from Lansdowne House.
The letter fairly explains itself.]

Baths of Leuk. Sept^{ber} 29, 1848.

My dear Clough

A woodfire is burning in the grate and I have been forced
to drink champagne to guard against the cold and the café
noir is about to arrive, to enable me to write a little. For I
am all alone in this vast hotel: and the weather having been
furious rain for the last few days, has tonight turned itself
towards frost. Tomorrow I repass the Gemmi and get to
Thun: linger one day at the Hotel Bellevue for the sake of
the blue eyes of one of its inmates: and then proceed by
slow stages down the Rhine to Cologne, thence to Amiens
and Boulogne and England.

The day before yesterday I passed the Simplon—and
yesterday I repassed it. The day before yesterday I lay at
Domo d'Ossola and yesterday morning the old man within
me and the guide were strong for proceeding to the Lago
Maggiore: but no, I said, first impressions must not be
trifled with: I have but 3 days and they, according to the
public voice will be days of rain: coupons court à notre
voyage —revenons en Suisse—So I ordered a char yesterday
morning to remount the Simplon. It rained still . . . here
and there was something unblurred by rain. Précisons: I
have noticed in Italy—the chestnuts: the vines: the courtli-
ness and kingliness of buildings and people as opposed to
this land of a republican peasantry: and one or two things
more: but d—n description. My guide assures me he saw
one or two 'superbes filles' in Domo d'Ossola (nothing im-
proper): but I rose late and disheartened by the furious rain,
and saw nothing but what I saw from the carriage. So Italy
remains for a second entry. From Isella to Simplon the
road is glory to God. In these rains maps and guides have

suffered more or less: but your Keller very little: I travel with a live guide as well as Murray: an expensive luxury: but if he is a good Xtian and a family man like mine, a true comfort. I gave him today a foulard for his daughter who is learning French at Neufchatel to qualify her first for the place of fille de chambre in a hotel and afterwards for that of soubrette in a private family. I love gossip and the small-wood of humanity generally among these raw mammoth-belched half-delightful objects the Swiss Alps. The lime stone is terribly gingerbready: the pines terribly larchy: and above all the grand views being ungifted with self-controul almost invariably desinunt in piscem. And the curse of the dirty water—the real pain it occasions to one who looks upon water as the Mediator between the inani-mate and man is not to be described.—I have seen clean water in parts of the lake of Geneva (w[hi]ch whole locality is spoiled by the omnipresence there of that furiously flaring bethiefed rushlight, the vulgar Byron):[1] in the Aar at the exit of the Lac de Thoune: and in the little stream's be-ginnings on the Italian side of the Simplon. I have how-ever done very little, having been baffled in two main wishes—the Tschingel Glacier and the Monte Moro, by the weather. My golies, how jealous you would have been of the first: 'we fools accounted his calves meagre, and his legs to be without honor'. All I have done however is to ascend the Faulhorn—8300 above the sea, my duck.

This people, the Swiss, are on the whole what they should be; so I am satisfied.—L'homme sage ne cherche point le sentiment parmi les habitans des montagnes: ils ont quelque chose de mieux—le bonheur. That is but indifferent French though. For their extortion, it is all right I think—as the wise man pumpeth the fool, who is made for to be pumped.

I have with me only Beranger and Epictetus: the latter[2] tho: familiar to me, yet being Greek, when tired I am, is not much read by me: of the former I am getting tired. Horace whom he resembles had to write only for a circle of highly cultivated desillusionés roués, in a sceptical age: we have the sceptical age, but a far different and wider audience: voilà pourquoi, with all his genius, there is something 'fade' about Beranger's Epicureanism. Perhaps you don't see the pourquoi, but I think my love does and the paper draws to an end. In the reste, I am glad to be tired of an author: one link in the immense series of cognoscenda et indagenda despatched. More particularly is this my feeling with regard to (I hate the word) women. We know beforehand all they can teach us: yet we are obliged to learn it directly from them. Why here is a marvellous thing. The following is curious—

'Say this of her:
The day was, thou wert not: the day will be,
Thou wilt be most unlovely: shall I chuse
Thy little moment life of loveliness
Betwixt blank nothing and abhorred decay
To glue my fruitless gaze on, and to pine,
Sooner than those twin reaches of great time,
When thou art either nought, and so not loved,
Or somewhat, but that most unloveable,
That preface and post-scribe thee?'— [3]

Farewell, my love, to meet I hope at Oxford: not alas in Heaven: tho: thus much I cannot but think: that our spirits retain their conquests: that from the height they succeed in raising themselves to, they can never fall. Tho: this uti possedetes principle may be compatible with entire loss of individuality and of the power to recognize one another. Therefore, my well-known love, accept my heartiest greeting and farewell, while it is called today.

Yours,
M. ARNOLD.

[1] In spite of the high service Arnold did Byron in making a selection of his poems and showing where his real power lay, he saw clearly 'the deep grain of coarseness and commonness, his affectation, his brutal selfishness' (Essay on Shelley, *Essays in Criticism*, 2nd series, p. 238). But the person 'who stops at the theatrical preludings does not know him' (Essay on Byron, *Essays*, 2nd series, p. 197). And Arnold's reflections on Heine, in 1863, were to persuade him that Byron, for all his weaknesses, was 'the greatest natural force, the greatest elementary power . . . in our literature since Shakspeare' (*Essays in Criticism*, 1st series, p. 192).

[2] Epictetus is mentioned also in the early sonnet, *To a Friend* (see *Poems*, p. 40, and in these Letters No. 21). For other references to

his work, see the essay on Wordsworth, *Essays in Criticism*, 2nd series, p. 145, and on Marcus Aurelius, *Essays*, 1st series, pp. 347–8, as well as 'A Speech at Eton', *Mixed Essays*, &c., p. 409.

³ The 'curious' thing is unquestionably Arnold's own. I was interested to find it scribbled, with one minor change, in the back of his copy of Burnett's *Life of Matthew Hale*. The thought is very close to that of the last part of the 'Horatian Echo'.

23

[The *Bothie* was published early in November. But it is the news of Lord Lansdowne's ('my man') having the gout at Bowood that enables the date of the letter to be fixed at not earlier than November 15. Lord Lansdowne left London for Bowood Park, his Wiltshire home, on November 13, and returned to town on Wednesday, December 6. See Court Circulars of *Times*, November 15 and December 8.

The rather mysterious first paragraph may concern the examinations at Oxford which Arnold's brother Edward was enduring, or negotiations for a position for Clough in the Education Office. It possibly refers, however, to the failure of Arthur Stanley to obtain, early in November 1848, the Professorship of Modern History at Oxford. Dr. Arnold had dreamed of Stanley as his own successor to that chair. Offering himself for the place largely at the instigation of Temple and Jowett, Stanley found his orthodoxy too strongly suspected. Henry Halford Vaughan was elected.]

London. Wednesday.
My dear Clough   [November (15, 22, or 29?), 1848]

Who had the clearest insight into the way in which business proceeded in the schools? That you, who have never had or acquired the art of correcting your individual judgement of merit by an appreciation of the circumstances that weigh with the world, in matters where the result is in the world's hands, should have so erred, does not surprize me: but that Walrond who, being more worldly than you, should have some tact, coincided with you in so monstrous a notion as yours, surprized, nay nettled me to a degree that required all the self-controul I muster when really nettled to conceal. Tell him this: and beg him to cultivate that finesse in his judgements, which it is so easy to lose. I hear from London thro: Shephard that Edward's Ethic

94

paper was marked with the first class mark.[1] Nor does this surprize me, though I do not account him therefore a philosopher.

—I have been at Oxford the last two days and hearing Sellar[2] and the rest of that clique who know neither life nor themselves rave about your poem gave me a strong almost bitter feeling with respect to them, the age, the poem, even you. Yes I said to myself something tells me I can, if need be, at last dispense with them all, even with him: better that, than be sucked for an hour even into the Time Stream in which they and he plunge and bellow. I became calm in spirit, but uncompromising, almost stern. More English than European, I said finally, more American than English: and took up Obermann,[3] and refuged myself with him in his forest against your Zeit Geist.

—But in another way I am glad to be able to say that Macpherson[4] gave a very good account of the sale: and that, tho: opinions differed, I found what I thought the best such as Riddell's[5] and Blackett's in favor of the metre strongly: the opinion of the first has a scientific that of the second an aesthetic value. Stanley thought him the best Hexameter he had seen in the modern languages. My people at home could not manage the metre, but thought there was humour and pathos enough in the poem to stock a dozen ordinary poems. I was surprized to see no notice in any Sunday papers: but next Sunday, I suppose. You will be glad to hear Conington[6] intends to review it. I bantered him gently about a discovery he had made in one of your lyrics of a resemblance to one of Tennyson's, which I never saw, and I do not think you either. Say to Shairp[7] I have seen a copy of Visconti just like mine: same price: £4–4[s]. does he want it? If not he does Walrond. Let me know pray. When are you coming up hither love? My man has the gout at Bowood.

yours ever
M. A.

[1] Edward Arnold received, however, only a third class *in literis humanioribus* for Michaelmas term. (*Times* of November 29.) The reference is doubtless to Thomas Henry Sheppard, one of Dr. Arnold's boys at Rugby. He matriculated at Oriel College in 1832. Later

fellow of Exeter College, and chaplain, 1851–88. (Foster, *Alumni Oxon.* (1715–1886), p. 1287.)

[2] William Yonge Sellar (1825–90), the classical scholar, and Arnold's good friend, was then a fellow at Oriel. (For Arnold's own opinion of the *Bothie*, see *On Translating Homer*, pp. 213 ff., 231.) Professor Sellar wrote a long article upon Clough for the *North British Review*, November 1862, pp. 323–43. He there, in his maturer judgement, still considers the *Bothie* 'the most lively and natural description of a phase of real modern life which we know of in English verse' (p. 336). But he also puts his finger upon what probably prevented Arnold from full enjoyment of the poem: 'The story of an Oxford reading-party in the Highlands of Scotland, one of the members of which falls three times in love in the course of six weeks, and finally marries Elspie, daughter of David M'Kay, blacksmith, and tenant of a bothie in Lochaber, could not, consistently with our ordinary associations, be treated in the grand style.'

[3] See Arnold's two treatments of Obermann in *Poems*, Oxford Standard Authors, pp. 174 ff. and 433 ff.

[4] Francis Macpherson, the Oxford publisher of the *Bothie*.

[5] James Riddell (1823–66), then fellow at Balliol and tutor there, had entered as Balliol scholar with Arnold. He became the distinguished classicist.

[6] John Conington (1825–69), classical scholar and translator of Virgil; then fellow of University College; afterwards Professor of Latin. (See also p. 142.)

[7] John Campbell Shairp (1819–85), close friend of Arnold and Clough at Balliol; at this time, a master of Rugby, where Clough is apparently visiting him. He was later principal of St. Andrews and Professor of Poetry at Oxford.

24

[This letter has nothing in it that fixes a definite date. The handwriting suggests strongly that it is of the 1848–9 period. The edition of Keats's life and letters by Monckton Milnes appeared in 1848. See review in *The Times*, September 19, p. 3. Milnes had been communicating with Clough about this work before it was published. I assume the publication date roughly fixes the time of this letter.

For the important light the letter sheds upon Arnold's own theory of poetry as a 'criticism of life', see Introduction, pp. 39–43.]

London. Monday. [after September 1848–9]

My dearest Clough

What a brute you were to tell me to read Keats' Letters. However it is over now: and reflexion resumes her power over agitation.

What harm he has done in English Poetry. As Browning[1] is a man with a moderate gift passionately desiring movement and fulness, and obtaining but a confused multitudinousness, so Keats with a very high gift, is yet also consumed by this desire: and cannot produce the truly living and moving, as his conscience keeps telling him. They will not be patient neither understand that they must begin with an Idea of the world in order not to be prevailed over by the world's multitudinousness: or if they cannot get that, at least with isolated ideas: and all other things shall (perhaps) be added unto them.

—I recommend you to follow up these letters with the Laocoön of Lessing:[2] it is not quite satisfactory, and a little mare's nesty—but very searching.

—I have had that desire of fulness without respect of the means, which may become almost maniacal: but nature had placed a bar thereto not only in the conscience (as with all men) but in a great numbness in that direction. But what perplexity Keats Tennyson et id genus omne must occasion to young writers of the ὁπλίτης* sort: yes and those d——d Elizabethan poets generally. Those who cannot read G[ree]k sh[ou]ld read nothing but Milton[3] and parts of Wordsworth: the state should see to it: for the failures of the σταθμοί† may leave them good citizens enough, as Trench: but the others go to the dogs failing or succeeding.

So much for this inspired 'cheeper' as they are saying on the moon.

My own good man farewell.

M. A.

[1] For other opinions on Browning, see pp. 51, 136; on Keats, see pp. 52, 100, 124, 126.

[2] The *Epilogue to Lessing's Laocoön* had at least been suggested by this time.

[3] So, two months before his death, he says: 'In our race are thousands of readers, presently there will be millions, who know not a word of Greek and Latin, and will never learn these languages. If

---

* 'heavy-armed foot soldier',

† 'march of the day'; in plural here it means 'stages along the royal road'.

this host of readers are ever to gain any sense of the power and charm of the great poets of antiquity, their way to gain it is not through translations of the ancients, but through the original poetry of Milton, who has the like power and charm, because he has the like great style. . . . Milton has made the great style no longer an exotic here: he has made it an inmate amongst us, a leaven, and a power.' ('Milton', *Essays in Criticism*, 2nd series, pp. 66–7.)

25

[The winter of 1848–9 Clough spent chiefly at Oxford and at his home in Liverpool, although he was occasionally at London to arrange for taking the Headship of University Hall, to which he had been invited. The institution, although connected with London University, was non-sectarian and, unlike Oxford, required no subscription. Clough's tenure was not to begin, however, until October 1849.

Meantime, in January 1849, he issued, with his friend Burbidge, the little volume of poems called *Ambarvalia*. See the advertisement for it in *The Times*, supplement, January 19, 1849.

The date of the letter is fixed more truly, however, by the way it relates to letter No. 26 (cf. prefatory comment, p. 100).

Arnold's criticism of Clough's poems, always frank and severe, reveals here some profound ideas, particularly important because they stress form and expression, and not moral qualities or thought, as the prime requisites of poetry. For his sensitiveness to the 'unpoetical age' and the adverse Zeitgeist, see pp. 32–3, 95, 98, 109–11, 122–3, 126, 130–1, 146.]

L[ansdowne] H[ouse]
Friday [early part of February 1849]

My dear Clough—

If I were to say the real truth as to your poems in general, as they impress me—it would be this—that they are not *natural*.

Many persons with far lower gifts than yours yet seem to find their natural mode of expression in poetry, and tho: the contents may not be very valuable they appeal with justice from the judgement of the mere thinker to the world's general appreciation of naturalness—i.e.—an absolute propriety—of form, as the sole *necessary* of Poetry as such: whereas the greatest wealth and depth of matter is merely a superfluity in the Poet *as such*.

—Form of Conception comes by nature certainly, but is generally developed late: but this lower form, of expression, is found from the beginning amongst all born poets, even feeble thinkers, and in an unpoetical age: as Collins, Green[e] and fifty more, in England only.

The question is not of congruity between conception and expression: which when both are poetical, is the poet's highest result:—you say what you mean to say: but in such a way as to leave it doubtful whether your mode of expression is not quite arbitrarily adopted.

I often think that even a slight gift of poetical expression which in a common person might have developed itself easily and naturally, is overlaid and crushed in a profound thinker so as to be of no use to him to help him to express himself.—The trying to go into and to the bottom of an object instead of grouping *objects* is as fatal to the sensuousness of poetry as the mere painting, (for, *in Poetry*, this is not *grouping*) is to its airy and rapidly moving life.

'Not deep the Poet sees, but wide':[1]—think of this as you gaze from the Cumner Hill toward Cirencester and Cheltenham.

—You succeed best you see, in fact, in the hymn, where man, his deepest personal feelings being in play, finds poetical expression as *man* only, not as artist:—but consider whether you attain the *beautiful*, and whether your product gives PLEASURE, not excites curiosity and reflexion. Forgive me all this: but I am always prepared myself to give up the attempt, on conviction: and so, I know, are you: and I only urge you to reflect whether you are advancing. Reflect too, as I cannot but do here more and more, in spite of all the nonsense some people talk, how deeply *unpoetical* the age and all one's surroundings are. Not unprofound, not ungrand, not unmoving:—but *unpoetical*.

Ever yrs
M. A.

[1] The line is quoted from Arnold's own *Resignation* and concludes a long section about the poet's nature that should be read in connexion

with this letter. We now know that the poem carries Arnold's deep
conviction of the sentiments he here describes. It is not merely
youthful music when he says of the true bard:

> Before him he sees life unroll,
> A placid and continuous whole—
> That general life, which does not cease,
> Whose secret is not joy, but peace.

26

[Arnold's first volume, *The Strayed Reveller, and other Poems*,
'by A.', was advertised in *The Times* of Monday, February 26,
1849 (Supplement, p. 10). The felicitations from his Oxford
friends must have come, therefore, about March 1.

Moreover, the date of this letter is fixed by the reference to
John Duke Coleridge. In a letter of Coleridge written
February 27, 1849, one finds: 'A little volume of poems came
to me yesterday "from the author", written by "A", published
by *Fellowes*. So I wrote to Matthew Arnold and asked him
to convey my thanks to "A", as Sir Walter Scott used to the
"Author of Waverley". They are, some of them, very beautiful—I think one or two better than any I have seen this long
while.' *The Life and Correspondence of John Duke Lord Coleridge*,
i. 190.

Also the sentence, 'It is true about form: something of the
same sort is in my letter which crossed yours on the road',
shows the connexion with the letter immediately before.]

[London?] [about March 1, 1849]
Dear Clough

The Iliad translation is better,[1] but not anglicised enough
I think. I am told that Germans who are ignorant of the
original complain that they cannot understand Voss.
Carlyle's Dante seemed to me clearer.

—It is true about form: something of the same sort is in my
letter which crossed yours on the road. On the other hand,
there are two offices of Poetry—one to add to one's store of
thoughts and feelings—another to compose and elevate
the mind by a sustained tone, numerous allusions, and a
grand style. What other process is Milton's than this last,
in Comus for instance. There is no fruitful analysis of
character: but a great effect is produced. What is Keats?

A style and form seeker, and this with an impetuosity that heightens the effect of his style almost painfully. Nay in Sophocles what is valuable is not so much his contributions to psychology and the anatomy of sentiment, as the grand moral effects produced by *style*. For the style is the expression of the nobility of the poet's character, as the matter is the expression of the richness of his mind: but on men character produces as great an effect as mind.[2]

This however does not save Burbidge who planes and polishes to the forgetting of matter without ever arriving at style. But my Antigone supports me and in some degree subjugates destiny.[3]

—I have had a very enthusiastic letter from Brodie[4] and from John Coleridge, to my surprize. These are all I have heard from. Shairp is δεξιά.[5]

Yours,

M. A.

[1] Clough's attempts at translating Homer are also mentioned in the next several letters. They were kept up to the end of his life. For specimens of his work, see *Poems*, 417–21. It is likely that his early efforts stimulated Arnold's own interest in Homeric translation and the later lectures on the subject. At the close of his last lecture, Arnold mentioned Clough's work in this field (*Last Words, &c.*, pp. 299–300).

[2] It is worth observing that what is said about the effect of a poet's character upon his style is incorporated in Arnold's definition: 'The grand style arises in poetry when *a noble nature*, poetically gifted, treats with simplicity or with severity a serious subject'. (*Last Words on Translating Homer*, p. 265).

[3] The tribute to Sophocles and his supporting power recalls the praise of him in the sonnet, *To a Friend*, and in the lecture *On the Modern Element in Literature*.

[4] Later Sir Benjamin Collins Brodie (1817–80), the distinguished Professor of Chemistry, at Oxford. He was also an old student at Balliol and Arnold's warm friend.

[5] i.e. 'on the right side'.

27

[The fragment which is here printed separately was doubtless enclosed in one of the letters of this time. Its date is fixed by the content.

The *Guardian* for the week of February 28, 1849 (pp. 145 6), contained a testimonial of a volume of poems by the Hon. Henry Robert Skeffington. The review gives the facts of the poet's life. The eighth child of the late Viscount Ferrard, he became a commoner of Worcester College, Oxford, in 1841, and was graduated in 1843. He died at Rome, February 17, 1846, in his twenty-second year.

Observe how Arnold's comments on Christian rapture coincide with what he says of religious warmth in Letter 48. The reference of 'desire to subjugate destiny' repeats the phrase used about *Antigone* in the preceding letter, with which this fragment was probably enclosed.]

[London? about Feb. 28, 1849]

If you can, get the Guardian of this week, to see a notice of some poems by that Skeffington who was at Worcester, and always at the Union and who afterwards died at Rome at 22. There is one on the Etruscan tombs of Perugia and Chiusi in which the following lines occur respecting the old Etruscans.

'Is all silent? know we nothing? Can Philosophy not rear
Some dim theoretic ages from the social fossils here?
And, amid the frightful clashing of her after-ages wild,
Hath the old world clean forgotten those who tended her, a child?
They are gone!—like sea-shore footsteps when the tide flows,—they are gone!
Swept by Heaven-won Regillus, swept by fatal Vadimon.
Swept, poor prisoners of Sorrow, to the doubtful dusk of death,
That another generation might be told the name of Faith.
Ah! for grief! what anguish took them when the fetter'd soul look'd out,
Straining aching eye in vain to pierce the curtain of their doubt!
Ah! for grief! what longing seiz'd it, to have wings and wander hence,
As the torn soul in its frenzy batter'd on the seas of sense!
Ah! for grief! what curse was knowledge! what a burden was the mind!
Better be a beast—go, fat thee, feed, and propagate thy kind!' &c. &c.

—I have abridged: whereby it gains: but what a true fire! although the union of a freedom from all desire to subjugate destiny with the natural fire of youth produces a state in which astonishing results can be produced compared with what can be produced early by the unintoxicated honest. He is a rapturous Xtian.

28

[The date of this letter and that of the little scrap placed after it are fixed by the obvious connexions with letter No. 27. Moreover, Arnold continues to mention letters received from friends about his first volume of poetry.]

[London?] Saturday [March 1849]

Dear Clough—

First for your matters.—I do not know the Iliad sufficiently well to give an opinion as to translating a portion: but before the end of April I shall know it well I hope.

—Your passage today is plainer: but not, I think, quite the thing, somehow. It is still too hard. Even things like *ordainer* Zeus would not be relished. You somehow keep too near the Greek sentence-form. Read the Bible: Isaiah, Job. &c.

—I should print in lines, as it makes it look easier: without the least scruple about placing opposite a Greek line an English one great part of which belonged to some other Greek line: if it is to be more than a *cab*, you must *Anglicise*, and this in the *form* above all. It is quite consistent with literalness so to do. And put paragraphs as often as they occur in Dindorf. This too conduces to plainness.

—As to 'anger fierce' I think the rule is to use English inversions and not G[ree]k ones. The inversion in question is I think a G[ree]k one. But there is no lack of them in English. Again consult the Bible.[1] Milton uses Greek and Latin structures for sentences, but then these sentences are comprehended within an *English metre-form*, which saves the impression of the *whole* from being foreign. But in prose you have no such counter-balance-means to a system of UnEnglishly constructed sentences. Βοῶπις large or full eyed: because we do not use the image in England: saucereyed and other-eyeds there are, amongst which you may perhaps find one that serves. For large-eyed is a shirking the word: though ox-eyed is unallowable as not English.— Drat Hexameters.[2] Try a bit in the metre I took for the sick king.

—For myself: Cumin[3] also advises a running commentary for the New Sirens: and Shairp finds them cloudy and obscure: and they are, what you called them, a mumble.

—*Yet* would be better than *Ah* in the passage you mention: It *expresses* the connection, which is now left to be perceived.

I must hear some day how you feel about Resignation. Tell me freely if you do not like it.

Goldwin Smith[4] likes the classical ones: but they hinder females from liking the book: and Shairp[5] urges me to speak more from myself: which I less and less have the inclination to do: or even the power.

yours sincerely,
M. ARNOLD.

[1] In his talks *On Translating Homer* (p. 220) he again recommends the Bible as 'the one English book and one only, where, as in the Iliad itself, perfect plainness of speech is allied with perfect nobleness'.

[2] But in his later Oxford lectures it is the hexameter he favours as the measure most likely to render the *Iliad* into English.

[3] Patrick Cumin, barrister, and one time secretary to W. E. Forster, had been Arnold's friend at Balliol.

[4] Goldwin Smith (1823–1910), historian and teacher, whose life was divided between England and America, at Oxford, Cornell, and Toronto. He and Arnold were to have long association. See Arnold's answer to Smith's defence of the Puritan middle classes (Essay on Equality, *Mixed Essays*, pp. 59–63); also the introduction to *Celtic Literature*, p. xviii. Also *Letters*, i. 157.

[5] Shairp (see p. 114, n. 3) was not at all reticent in his criticism of Arnold's poetry. In an undated letter to Clough, he says: 'I do not feel that great background of fatalism or call it what you will which is behind all his thoughts. But he thinks he sees his way.' As late as 1853, he regrets to see so much real power 'thrown away upon so false and uninteresting a view of life. . . . Since you have gone fr[om] England, it's yours you've gone to a hearty fresh young people, rather than into the "blank dejection of European Capitals". Anything that so takes the life from out things must be false. It's this I like about your things that tho' in theory you maintain the contrary, yet in fact the "great human heart" will out and you can't hinder it. Stick to this. Mat, as I told him, disowns man's natural feelings, and they will disown his poetry. If there's nothing else in the world but blank dejections, it's not worth while setting them to music.' (Clough MSS.)

29

[London?] Saturday [about March, 1849]

Much better, I think.

Be easy, easy. Ἐπὶ ξυροῦ ἀκμῆς *

has not an English equivalent, literal, as you put it. Think
of something else. 'Generian horseman' is a bad *style* of
thing—Put articles—The horseman of Gerenia, I should
say, to avoid obscurity. *A single thing* is not *strown.* 'Yes, in
all this etc.' is a truly Cloughian line: a little too much so.

Yours

M. A.

30

[The abrupt beginning is Arnold's running commentary for
The New Sirens, which he has been prompt to furnish after
Clough's suggestion. See the previous letter. He is still receiving
letters about his poems.]

[March, 1849]

The *New* Sirens

A lawn stretching away in front of the palace of the New
Sirens, dotted with pines and cedars, and with glimpses to
the right and left over the open country. Time evening.

The speaker (one of a band of poets) stands under a
cedar, newly awakened from a sleep: the New Sirens are
seen round about in their bowers in the garden, dejected.

He addresses them, saying he has dreamed they were =
the Sirens the fierce sensual lovers of antiquity.

Yet, he says, this romantic place, and the multitude and
distinction of your worshippers some of them attracted
from the service of the spirit by you, seem to indicate a
higher worth in you. Are you then really something better
and more lawfully attractive than the old Sirens?

—oh, he continues, I perceive the change that gives you
an advantage over them. Your love is romantic, and claims
to be a satisfying of the spirit.

And, he says, I cannot argue against you: for when about

* See *Iliad* x. 173.

to do so, the remembrance of your beauty and life as I witnessed it at sunrise on these lawns occupies my mind, and stops my mouth.

—Yes, he continues, that was glorious: and if that could have lasted, or if we were so made as not to feel that it did not last—(aposiopesis)

—But, soon after the life and enjoyment I witnessed in you at day-break, a languor fell upon you as the day advanced: the weather clouded, your happy groups were broken up, and in lassitude and ennui you dispersed yourselves thro: the gardens, and threw yourselves dispiritedly down in your bowers where at evening I now see you.

—Does the remembrance of your vivacity of this morning suffice to console you in the void and weariness of the afternoon and evening? or do your thoughts revert to that life of the spirit to which, like me, you were once attracted, but which, finding it hard and solitary, you soon abandoned for the vehement emotional life of passion as 'the new Sirens'?

What, he says, without reply, I see you rise and leave your bowers, and re-enter your palace. And yet do not be angry with me: for I would gladly find you in the right and myself, with my conscientious regrets after the spiritual life, wrong.

(They have re-entered the palace, and night falls)

—That is right, he continues, away with ennui, and let joy revive amidst light and dancing.

—But, (after a pause he continues), I, remaining in the dark and cold under my cedar, and seeing the blaze of your revel in the distance, do not share your illusions: and ask myself whether this *alternation* of ennui and excitement is worth much? Whether it is in truth a very desirable life?

And, he goes on, were this *alternation* of ennui and excitement the best discoverable existence, yet it cannot last: time will destroy it: the time will come, when the elasticity of the spirits will be worn out, and nothing left but weariness.

(This epoch is described under the figure of morning but all this latter part you say is clear to you.)

I have thus, my love, ventured to trouble you with a sort

of argument to the poem, thanking you for the trouble you
seem to have bestowed on it.

But your word is quite just—it is exactly a mumble[1]—
and I have doctored it so much and looked at it so long
that I am now powerless respecting it.

I believe you are right about the shuttle[2] also: but I will
look in the technological dict: one is sadly loose by default
of experience, about spinning and weaving, with a great
poetical interest in both occupations.

Brodie's letter pleased me very much: Wall[3] tells me he
thinks the poems really very pretty—especially (notwith-
standing its odd title) the Merman.

Goodbye my love

M. ARNOLD.—

[1] *The New Sirens* was removed from the next edition. Upon Swin-
burne's entreaty, it was revised in 1876, reprinted in *Macmillan's
Magazine* for December of that year.

[2] Lines 96–7 of *The Forsaken Merman* now stand:

Till the *spindle drops* from her hand,
And the whizzing wheel stands still.

But 'spindle drops' reads 'shuttle falls' until 1869.

[3] Henry Wall, former fellow of Balliol and then a lecturer on Logic;
from 1849, Wykeham Professor of Logic. For Brodie, see p. 101, note 4.

31

[What would seem to be the only existing letter from Clough
to Arnold falls next into our series. It is printed in full here
from the manuscript, because it is given only in part in Clough's
Prose Remains, pp. 160–1.

As the work at University Hall did not start until October
1849, Clough left in April for Rome, where he saw Mazzini
and his associates endure, and finally succumb to, the siege
of the French under General Oudinot. Forced to remain in
Rome until the first part of July, he occupied himself with his
long *Amours de Voyage*.]

Rome. June 23rd [1849]

Dear Matt

Why the d—l I shd write to you he only knows who
implanted the spirit of disinterested attention in the heart
of the spaniel—

Parliament breaks up at the end of July—or even earlier saith Galignani—Our orbits therefore early in August might perhaps cross, and we two serene undeviating stars salute each other once again for a moment amid the infinite spaces—Not that I particularly desire or any way urge such an event—but I advertise you that I hope to be in the Geneva country about that time—reposing in the bosom of Nature from the fatigues of Art and the turmoil of War!!!!

Quid Romae faciam? What's Politics to he or he to Politics? But it is impossible to get out, and if one did, Freeborn, Vice Consul, who however is a *Caccone*, says the French avanposti shoot at once.

June 28th.

Rather warm work in both senses. I shall send this enclosed to Palgrave*. Will it find you still in the hot streets? I hope within ten days more at any rate to get off. The City may hold out that long. The day after tomorrow completes the month of siege.—

I *believe* St. Peters etc. are not mined.—I was told that Canino had affirmed it in Mazzini's presence without contradiction: but Avezzana Mʳ of War most positively denies it to the American banker, who lives in our house here.—

July 3 Tuesday.

Well, we are taken; the battery immediately to the left (as you go out) of San Pancrazio was [taken] carried by assault on the night of the 29th or morning of the 30th rather, while we in this corner got bombarded by way of feint.—The Roman line in several cases has behaved ill, and certainly gave way here rather early; afterwards however under Garibaldi's command it seems to have fought well—at least two regiments, which are now off with him and his free corps to the Abruzzi.

On Saturday evening the Assembly resolved to give in: Mazzini & Co. resigned; and a deputation went off to Oudinot. Sunday was perfectly tranquil—Yesterday evening Garibaldi withdrew his troops from the Trastevere and went off by the S. Giovanni. Today they say the French will enter. Altogether I incline to think the Roman popu-

* This sentence crossed out.

lation *has* shown a good deal of 'apathy'—they didn't care about the bombs much, but they didn't care to fight *very* hard, either. The Lombards are fine fellows;—and the Bolognese too.—The only pity there were not more of them. —If you put the whole lot of them together—Poles, Lombards, Tuscans, French, they w[ou]ld not exceed 3000 I sh[ou]ld think at the very utmost—.

There is very little harm done by the bombarding—On the whole the French were not very barbarious, but if we hadn't yielded I believe they meant to bombard us *really*, and as it was, their shells might have done some irreparable harm.—

A. H. C.

At noon today the Assembly proclaims the Constitution! —which it had just completed.

I shall stay just to see these blackguards behave and then cut north.

———

32

[The proposed meeting at Geneva evidently did not take place. The long interval of absence was justified, however, if only for its inducing this really remarkable letter. It makes its own meaning clear; and it brings us as close to the young Arnold, the poet, as does anything I know.]

Thun. Sunday. Sept^{ber} 23 [1849]

My dear Clough

I wrote to you from this place last year. It is long since I have communicated with you and I often think of you among the untoward generation with whom I live and of whom all I read testifies. With me it is curious at present: I am getting to feel more independent and unaffectible as to all intellectual and poetical performance the impatience at being faussé in which drove me some time since so strongly into myself, and more snuffing after a moral atmosphere to respire in than ever before in my life. Marvel not that I say unto you, ye must be born again. While I will not much talk of these things, yet the considering of them has led me constantly to you the only living one almost that I know of of

> The children of the second birth
> Whom the world could not tame— [1]

for my dear Tom has not sufficient besonnenheit for it to be any *rest* to think of him any more than it is a *rest* to think of mystics and such cattle—not that Tom is in any sense cattle or even a mystic but he has not a 'still, considerate mind'. [2]

What I must tell you is that I have never yet succeeded in any one great occasion in consciously mastering myself: I can go thro: the imaginary process of mastering myself and see the whole affair as it would then stand, but at the critical point I am too apt to hoist up the mainsail to the wind and let her drive. However as I get more awake to this it will I hope mend for I find that with me a clear almost palpable intuition (damn the logical senses of the word) is necessary before I get into prayer: unlike many people who set to work at their duty self-denial etc. like furies in the dark hoping to be gradually illuminated as they persist in this course. Who also perhaps may be sheep but not of my fold, whose one natural craving is not for profound thoughts, mighty spiritual workings etc. etc. but a distinct seeing of my way as far as my own nature is concerned: which I believe to be the reason why the mathematics were ever foolishness to me. [3]

—I am here in a curious and not altogether comfortable state: however tomorrow I carry my aching head to the mountains and to my cousin the Bhunlis Alp.

> Fast, fast by my window
> The rushing winds go
> Towards the ice-cumber'd gorges,
> The vast fields of snow.
> There the torrents drive upward
> Their rock strangled hum,
> And the avalanche thunders
> The hoarse torrent dumb.
> I come, O ye mountains—
> Ye torrents, I come, [4]

Yes, I come, but in three or four days I shall be back here, and then I must try how soon I can ferociously turn towards England.

My dearest Clough these are damned times—everything is against one—the height to which knowledge is come, the spread of luxury, our physical enervation, the absence of great *natures*, the unavoidable contact with millions of small ones, newspapers, cities, light profligate friends, moral desperadoes like Carlyle,⁵ our own selves, and the sickening consciousness of our difficulties: but for God's sake let us neither be fanatics nor yet chalf blown by the wind but let us be ὡς ο φρονιμος διαρισειεν and not as any one else διαρισειεν.*⁶ When I come to town I tell you beforehand I will have a real effort at managing myself as to newspapers and the talk of the day. Why the devil do I read about L d. Grey's sending convicts to the Cape,⁷ and excite myself thereby, when I can thereby produce no possible good. But public opinion consists in a multitude of such excitements. Thou fool—that which is morally worthless remains so, and undesired by Heaven, whatever results flow from it. And which of the units which has felt the excitement caused by reading of Lord Grey's conduct has been made one iota a better man thereby, or can honestly call his excitement a *moral* feeling.

You will not I know forget me. You cannot answer this letter for I know not how I come home.

Yours faithfully,

M. A.

¹ From his own 'Stanzas in Memory of the Author of Obermann', which he was then writing (see *Poems*, p. 178):

> For thou art gone away from earth,
> And place with those dost claim,
> The Children of the Second Birth,
> Whom the world could not tame; . . .

² Although there was always a deep and real affection between Arnold and his brother Tom, their intellectual differences were notorious in the family. One can hardly imagine the author of *Literature and Dogma* ever following Newman into the Catholic Church, although the power and attraction of that church he saw strongly.

* See note 6 for translation.

The depth of religious feeling this letter reveals is genuine, but of another sort. It belongs to him who wrote sometime later: 'I think, as Goethe thought, that the right thing is . . . to keep pushing on one's posts into the darkness, and to establish no post that is not perfectly in light and firm' (*Letters*, i. 289). For further consideration of Arnold's religious views, see Introduction, pp. 4, 24, 35–6, 49–52.

³ Recalling one of their early tutors, Tom Arnold wrote, 'Euclid he taught us also; but here the natural bent of my brother's mind showed itself. Ratiocination did not at that time charm him; and the demonstration of what he did not care to know found him languid' (*Passages in a Wandering Life*, p. 10). One of Matthew Arnold's worst hardships as inspector of schools was concocting the dull problems in arithmetic with which he would have to sweep down upon a class. His note-books are inked with entries from six great literatures; and scribbled over them in pencil are sums and problems painfully stored up against an evil hour.

⁴ This passage is incorporated into 'Parting', the second poem of the 'Switzerland' group (*Poems*, p. 190).

⁵ For comment on Carlyle and in respect of Arnold's complaint against the times, see Introduction, pp. 32–3, 47.

⁶ In his Greek phrases, Arnold is trying to suggest Aristotle's *Nicomachæan Ethics*, Book II. vi. 15: Ἔστιν ἄρα ἡ ἀρετὴ ἕξις προαιρετική, ἐν μεσότητι οὖσα τῇ πρὸς ἡμᾶς, ὡρισμένῃ λόγῳ καὶ ὡς ἂν ὁ φρόνιμος ὁρίσειε. 'Virtue, therefore, is a habit, accompanied with deliberate preference, in the relative mean, defined by reason, and as the prudent man would define it.' Arnold means, therefore: 'but let us be "as the prudent man would define", and not as any one else would "define"'.

⁷ Throughout the entire year of 1849, Earl Grey, the Colonial Minister, had been resisted in his plan to make the Cape of Good Hope a penal colony. (For a clear statement of his difficulties, see the *Annual Register*, 1849, pp. 371–5.) The *Examiner* for September 23 (p. 595) shows what importance the question had attained in England. Arnold's dislike of newspapers continued through his life. In 1851 he informs his sister, 'I have not looked at the newspapers for months, and when I hear of some dispute or rage that has arisen, it sounds quite historical; as if it was only the smiths at Ephesus being alarmed for their trade, when the Bishops remonstrate against Cardinal Wiseman's appearance; or Pompey blundering away his chances, when I hear of the King of Prussia, with such an army, getting himself and his country more shackled and *déconsidéré* every day.' (*Letters*, i. 18.)

33

[This letter is dated by its reference to the heated election at Rugby of a head master to take the place of Dr. Tait. The election occurred on November 18, 1849. Arnold has been on a visit to the school and is writing to Clough, now returned to his duties at University Hall in London.

Edward M. Goulburn (1819–97), later Dean of Norwich, who had known Arnold and Clough at school and at Oxford, was elected head master over William Charles Lake (1817–97), later the Dean of Durham and particularly remembered as the close friend of Arthur Stanley. Goulburn stayed at Rugby eight years, but his policy was not the liberal one of Dr. Arnold and Dr. Tait. Rugby men, during his leadership, made brilliant records as scholars; but the attendance had so fallen off, that he was obliged to give up his post in 1857. Clough liked him, however, and wrote early in January 1850, 'As for Goulburn I really am very decently satisfied; think him very likely to be quite as good as Lake—he is really a worthy creature; and has got "a fond" of genial humanity under that evangelical reputation—I think you Masters will be very silly if you don't make the best of him without further complaining.' MS. letter to J. C. Shairp.]

[Rugby] [shortly before November 18, 1849]

Dear Clough

Lawley[1] called—stayed a vast while—and hindered my coming to wish you goodbye.

I have been to Thurleston with Walrond today— to Kenilworth tomorrow—don't you envy me.

I shall go to Bowood most likely at the beginning of next month. I will let you know when I am about to come thro: town.

They are very bitter agst Lake some of them: Price above all. Goulburn they say will be elected: the boys will blow their nose in his coat tails as he walks thro: the 4gle.

Yours in great haste
M. A.

Down again dressed for dinner—
after dinner to the Price's[2]—but thou'dst not think,
Horatio, how ill it is here—

I said a lovely poem to that fool Shairp today which he was incapable of taking in.[3] He is losing his hair. Tom has had an offer of the Inspectorship of schools in V. Diemen's land. £400 a year and his expenses: we hear from the Colonial office that this offer has been made by the Governor of V. Diemen's Land. Whether accepted or not

we don't know. I shouldn't wonder if he took it. I think I
shall emigrate: why the devil don't you.
I will send you the Homer travestied someday.

M. A.

[1] Stephen Lawley (1823–1905), later sub-dean of York; member
of Balliol college during Arnold's Oxford years, from 1846 as a fellow.
(Foster, *Alumni Oxon.* (1715–1886), p. 823.)

[2] Bonamy Price (1807–88), the economist; then mathematical
master at Rugby.

[3] Shairp has apparently been continuing to rag Arnold about the
art of poetry (see pp. 101, 104).

34

[This letter is dated by its reference to *Memorial Verses*, which
Arnold did at the request of Edward Quillinan, Wordsworth's
son-in-law and neighbour of the Arnold family at Fox How.
Wordsworth died April 23, 1850, and Arnold's poem was
published in *Fraser's Magazine* for June of that year. I take
the letter therefore to be of May 1850.

Quillinan wrote Crabb Robinson, asking him to call on
Arnold at 101 Mount Street, Piccadilly, and see 'a very clever
little poem on "The Death of Wordsworth". . . . It is *very*
classical,' he continues, 'or it would not be M. A.'s. . . . It is
a triple Epicede on your Friends Wordsworth and Goethe,
and on Byron who, I think, leaving other objections out of the
question, is not tall enough for the other two;—and you, who
have no taste for tri-unities will hardly approve this. But
M. Arnold has a good deal of poetry in him; and it will come
out in spite of all the heathen Gods and goddesses that hold
him in enchantment. . . .' *Crabb Robinson's Correspondence with
the Wordsworth Circle*, ii. 769.]

[London] Tuesday. [May 1850]

Dear Clough

Or my memory bewrayeth me or thou promisedst to
come and breakfast with me tomorrow morning. Maske-
lyne[1] has offered himself for that day: and two is to my
mind naught at breakfast—besides thou lovest not that
young man. Forster[2] wants to see you: come therefore on
Friday at 9¼ and you shall meet him. I am engaged the

evenings of this week: still I would fain see thee as I have
at Quillinan's sollicitation dirged W. W. *in the grand style*
and need thy rapture therewith.

F. Newman's book [3] I saw yestern at our ouse. He seems
to have written himself down an hass. It is a display of the
theological mind, which I am accustomed to regard as a
suffetation, existing in a man from the beginning, colouring
his whole being, and being him in short. One would think
to read him that enquiries into articles, biblical inspiration, etc. etc. were as much the natural functions of a man
as to eat and copulate. This sort of man is only possible in
Great Britain and North Germany, thanks be to God
for it. Ireland even spews him out.

The world in general has always stood towards religions
and their doctors in the attitude of a half-astonished clown
acquiescingly ducking at their grand words and thinking
it must be very fine, but for its soul not being able to make
out what it is all about. This beast talks of such matters as
if they were meat and drink. What a miserable place
Oxford and the society of the serious middle classes must
have been 20 years ago. He bepaws the religious sentiment
so much that he quite effaces it to me. This sentiment now,
I think, is best not regarded alone, but considered in conjunction with the grandeur of the world, love of kindred,
love, gratitude etc. etc.

Il faut feuilleter seulement cet ouvrage: wenn man es
durchlesen sollte, so wäre es gar zu eckelhaft.

yours dear

M. A.

[1] Mervin Herbert Nevil Storey, who assumed the name of Maske-
lyne, had been at Oxford as a member of Wadham College. He
became a student of the Inner Temple in 1846; later, professor of
mineralogy at Oxford. Foster, *Alumni Oxon.* (1715–1886), iii. 923.

[2] Arnold's elder sister Jane had married William Edward Forster.

[3] Francis Newman (1805–97), brother of John Henry Newman and
Professor of Latin at University College, London, was later party to
the famous controvery with Arnold over Homeric translation (see
Letter 55). His *Phases of Faith*, one of his many books upon religious
subjects, appeared in 1850, the year after he had written *The Soul*.
For the reflections on theology and religion that he sets going in
Arnold's mind, see pp. 49–52.

35

[There are naturally few letters during 1850 and 1851, for Clough and Arnold were together in London. Here they continued somewhat the intimacy of the old Oriel days. Arnold's MS. journal, now the property of Viscountess Sandhurst, shows that during 1851, until he married Frances Lucy Wightman, he breakfasted with Clough on an average twice a week.

In the autumn of 1850 Clough had taken a brief vacation in Venice. The news of his return to his work in London has just come to Arnold, now for a while at Rugby, after a trip of his own to the Continent.]

Rugby. October 23. [18]50

Dear Clough

So you are come back—I came to Rugby too late on Monday to find you.

Of your letters I naturally saw nothing—not having been at Geneva. I hope they were characterized by your usual laconism, and then the loss is the less. I could not write to you for ignorance of your orbit—nor did I want to much: I have often thought of you, however.

Walrond seems to have learned nothing of your late goings on: tell me what they have been—what you have chiefly meditated or performed—in what spirits you are and health, quod rerum omnium est primum, muth verloren alles verloren. In all religions the supreme Being is represented as eternally rejoicing.

I thought of you in a letter of Jacobi's [1] the other day— now for my best hand—Der ich ward der bin ich, gequält von meiner Kindheit an mit einem heimlichen unüberwindlichen Eckel an mir selbst, dem Menschen; so dass ich, immer mehr verarmt an Hoffnung, oft es kaum ertrage, so ein Ding zu seyn: eine Lüge, unter lauter Lügen; ein Geträume, von Geträumten; und wenn ich meyne wach zu seyn noch weniger als das.

I communicate this on the strength of Pliny's adage quoted in the same letter—Deus est mortali juvare mortalem.

I go to read Locke on the Conduct of the Understanding: my respect for the reason as the rock of refuge to this poor exaggerated surexcited humanity increases and increases.

Locke is a man who has cleared his mind of vain repetitions, though without the positive and vivifying atmosphere of Spinoza² about him. This last, smile as you will,
I have been studying lately with profit.

Yours
M. A.

here till Saturday.

¹ 'What I was I still am, troubled from my childhood up with a
secret unconquerable disgust with myself, a nobody; so that I, always
more impoverished in hope, often can hardly suffer the thought of the
thing I am; a lie among nothing but lies, a thing of dreams among
dream-things, and whenever I think I am awake I am still less than
that.' See *Briefwechsel zwischen Goethe und F. H. Jacobi*, Leipzig, 1846,
p. 70; letter number 24, dated April 28, 1784.

² He has already begun the reading of Spinoza which was to inspire
'The Bishop and the Philosopher' (*Macmillan's Magazine*, January,
1863) and the essay on 'Spinoza and the Bible' (*Essays in Criticism*,
1st series, pp. 307 ff.). In this last essay Arnold amplifies what he says
here about Spinoza's 'positive and vivifying atmosphere': 'To be
great, he [a philosopher] must have something in him which can
influence character, which is edifying; he must, in short, have a noble
and lofty character himself, a character—to recur to that much-
criticized expression of mine—*in the grand style*. This is what Spinoza
had; and because he had it, he stands out from the multitude of
philosophers, and has been able to inspire in powerful minds a feeling
which the most remarkable philosophers, without this grandiose
character, could not inspire . . . his foot is in the *vera vita*, his eye on the
beatific vision' (pp. 341 and 343). For a consideration of Spinoza's
contribution to Arnold's religious thought, see also pp. 50–1.

———

36

[In order to marry, Arnold took, on April 14, 1851, a post as
Inspector of Schools. In this work he was to continue for
thirty-five years.

Meanwhile, Clough had found the life at University Hall
not to his taste. At the end of 1851 he resigned his Principalship and applied for the head post at a new college in Sydney,
Australia. Among the letters of recommendation he secured
was one from Matthew Arnold, dated December 5, 1851.
It is an unusually valuable letter. It is printed in full in
Appendix V.

Clough did not get the Australian post, on the prospect of
which he had become engaged to Miss Blanche Smith, of

Combe Hurst, Surrey. His friends had been urging him meantime to try the Education Office. Arnold's next letter advises
on the proper way to use the name of Mr. Ralph Lingen, the
Secretary.]

Babington Hall. Derby.
Saturday [shortly after December 19, 1851]

My dear Clough

What with schools in the Pittener starting and 2 hours to
inspect, tooth ache and other incommodities I have been
sore put to it lately. I return your draft, which is of Doric
plainness, but perhaps is as good as any you could send.
Say 'Mr. Lingen.'—but you must previously mention to
him that you are place-hunting and use his name to the
extent you do. I am sincerely interested in this application
of yours, I need not say. I think an Inspectorship would be
better suited to you though than an Examinership, besides
the pay being better. Hard dull work low salary stationari-
ness, and London to be stationary in under such circumstances, do not please me. However I myself would gladly
have married under any circumstances, and so, I doubt
not, you feel.[1]—I really think with L[ad]y Ashburton's help[2]
and your own character, you have an excellent prospect of
getting *some* situation in the C. O. within the coming year.
But be bustling about it; we are growing old, and advancing
towards the deviceless darkness: it would be well not to
reach it till we had at least tried *some* of the things men
consider desirable.—I never see the Globe, but supposed
they would be glad of Ld. Palmerston's going,[3] as Blackett
was the only man on the journal who liked him.

I shall be in town next week and shall see you without
fail. Till then adieu.

Yours ever
M. A.

[1] Although he assumed his work as a means of support, he transformed it, as he did his others, into a thing of large issues and profound
considerations. Before he was through he brought into English education a new vision from the Continent and showed the place of the
State in these matters as no one had shown it before. By October 15,
1851, he is becoming somewhat adjusted: 'I think I shall get interested
in the schools after a little time; their effects on the children are so
immense, and their future effects in civilising the next generation of

the lower classes, who, as things are going, will have most of the political power of the country in their hands, may be so important.' (*Letters*, i. 20.)

² See p. 122.

³ The date of the letter is determined by the reference to Lord Palmerston, who was dismissed on December 19, 1851, from his place as Foreign Secretary, because of his having expressed himself favourably about the *coup d'état* of Louis Napoleon. The phrase 'within the coming year' suggests it is still December.

37

[There is hardly a question that Clough received the notion that Arnold was growing somewhat away from him. See the reply that Arnold makes to him in Letter 42, which explains the situation as it really stood. For a time, at least, the subject of any coolness is not broached. But Clough wrote Miss Smith in March 1852, 'Sunday 10 A.M. Tonight I go to the Blacketts (in the evening only) to meet Mr. and Mrs. Matt Arnold again; they leave town tomorrow. Considering that he is my most intimate friend (or has been) it is not a great deal to have seen of him during ten days that he has been here and hereabout, to have spent an hour with him at a theatre last evening: well perhaps a couple of hours more this evening at a party? What would you have thought of that between Miss Becker [Miss Smith's most intimate friend] and you? I like the wife very well,—more, the more I see of her; Nevertheless?—Sunday 10 P.M.—I have not gone to the Blacketts, for it has rained cats and dogs, and I had got wet through in going to see the Carlyles or rather coming back and was sick of it. I am rather sorry not to go but at nine o'clock it was desperate. And I did not like sending out the man to get wet through in finding the cab. Would that humane motive have kept you from flying to the company of Miss Becker?' (Clough MSS.)

At all events, he finally wrote to Arnold, who was away from London most of the time on inspecting duties. The letter Arnold sends in reply refers, I take it, to Clough's failure to appear upon another occasion at Mr. Justice Wightman's home in Eaton Place.]

3 Imperial Square, Cheltenham.
Good Friday. [April 9, 1852.]

My dear Clough

I have this morning received your note—to my great joy. I did not know what had become of you. Did they tell you

I called at Doubting Castle the very day you escaped from it. I took it very ill you did not come and dine that day in Eaton Place—the—ye have always with you, but me ye have not always. However all will be forgiven if you obey me now. From Rugby you will come and see me at Derby, at my expense.[1] You will come early on a Saturday morning and go back late on a Monday night. Now this must absolutely be, therefore resign yourself. I go to Derby on Tuesday, and shall be there some fortnight or three weeks.

I submit myself to the order of events and revolve with the solar system in general. Particulars when we meet.

O fool, port. means portable or pocket edition—and a beast of a book it must be. Capell's text is *painfully* faulty— so much so that a very moderately read Shakespearian detects something wrong every page. 'Their currents turn *away* instead of *awry*—and heaps more. But I stick to Homer.

Adieu and love me. Write by return of post to me *here*. I go on Tuesday morning. Kindest regards to Shairp. Flu sends her kind regards to you. I have a real craving to see you again. Tell me if you are likely to have anything to do. —How life rushes away, and youth. One has dawdled and scrupled and fiddle faddled—and it is all over. Adieu again my dear Clough

Your ever affectionate

Envelope addressed: M. A.
   A. H. Clough Esqre
   J. C. Shairp's Esqre Rugby

[1] On Easter morning, April 11, two days after this invitation, Clough again confides to his fiancée:
'If, as you say, Papa leaves on Friday, then I suppose I must go and see Matt Arnold who has written to press [*sic*] to come to him for Sunday at *Derby*.'

38

Ibstock British School. April 22nd 1852

My dear Clough
     I was sincerely disappointed not to see you: however I suppose it was inevitable. Let me know what you are doing, and what your prospects are.

With respect to literary employment much may be said
—I will mention one or two things.

1. An edition of the Greek lyric poets before Sophocles,
that should be *readable*. It should be in English and drenched
in flesh and blood—each poet's remains should be pre-
ceded by his life, and instead of repulsive references to Ath.
Stob. etc. it should be simply narrated under what circumstances we get each fragment, what is the character of
Athenaeus and Stobaeus's collections, in what context the
fragment comes etc. All this in English, as if you were
writing a book for educated persons interested in poetry,
and knowing Greek, to read. I could go on for ever with
this scheme—a delicious book might thus be made. Every
fragment should be followed by its literal prose English
translation.

2. The same for Theocritus[1] and his contemporaries—pre-
ceded by a history of the state of literature and the world
at that time

3. A judicious translation of Diog. Laertius, leaving out the
trash, and taking away the dry compilatory character of the
lives—making them living biographies so far as they go.

4. Lives of the English Poets from where Johnson ends—
and in his method: biographical but above this, *critical*:
presupposing detailed lives of each poet, and contracting
the whole.

I am going to lunch with a farmer. Adieu.

ever yours affly.

M. A.

Envelope addressed:
A. H. Clough Esq:[re]
Oxford & Cambridge Club
Pall Mall *London*

---

[1] The interest in Theocritus foreshadows Arnold's own future essay
on 'Pagan and Medieval Religious Sentiment', with its lively rendering
of the fifteenth idyll (*Essays in Criticism*, 1st series, pp. 194 ff.). For that
matter, *Thyrsis* itself is complete evidence of how thoroughly he was
steeped in the later Greek poetry. One of the most delightful memories
of Arnold's children is that of their father's chats upon Greek and
Roman antiquities before a winter fire. He had his own father's gift of
making history live again. Only when some one tried to impress him
by 'talking tall' of these matters would he keep profoundly silent.

39

[The appointment to the college at Sydney was not given to
Clough, and his salary as Professor of English at University
College was but thirty pounds a year. He had gained, however, the help of Lady Ashburton, which Arnold here advises
him to use. I have at hand the complete correspondence that
passed between Clough and his benefactress. Lady Ashburton
was untiring in her effort to see him properly provided with a
post at the Education Office. On Arnold's part, the letter
shows with new clearness how much under the influence of the
Time-Spirit he constantly was. His sense that the gifted and
talented had too often drawn within their ivory towers and
not helped the world prepares one somewhat for his later
adventures into religion and social theory.]

6. Goldsmiths Building
Frances St. Edgbaston
June 7th 1852

My dear Clough

I got your scrap today—at first I hesitated whether the
rejection was meant of the professorship or the other matter
—but it *must* be the former. On the whole, and considering
all you told me (supposing you told the truth, ce qui
n'arrive pas toujours en pareil cas) I can hardly bring
myself to be very deeply grieved. Write me a line and tell
me how it all was, and what you mean to do. If possible,
get something to do before your term at the Hall expires: living on
your resources waiting for something to turn up is a bad
and dispiriting business. I recommend you to make some
use of the Ashburtons: is it possible I could be of any service
to you under any circumstances by word pen or purse?
Think.

Au reste, a great career is hardly possible any longer—
can hardly now be purchased even by the sacrifice of repose dignity and inward clearness—so I call no man unfortunate. I am more and more convinced that the world
tends to become more comfortable for the mass, and more
uncomfortable for those of any natural gift or distinction—
and it is as well perhaps that it should be so—for hitherto

the gifted have astonished and delighted the world, but
not trained or inspired or in any real way changed it—
and the world might do worse than to dismiss too high pre-
tentions, and settle down on what it can see and handle
and appreciate. I am sometimes in bad spirits, but generally
in better than I used to be. I am sure however that in the
air of the present times il nous manque d'aliment, and
that we deteriorate in spite of our struggles—like a gifted
Roman falling on the uninvigorating atmosphere of the
decline of the Empire. Still nothing can absolve us from
the duty of doing all we can to keep alive our courage and
activity.

Written very late at night. Goodnight and keep alive,
my dear Clough.

yours cordially

M. A.

40

[Clough was now more than ever eager to get some employ-
ment whereby he might marry. On June 17, 1852, he wrote
Emerson asking if there were any chance of 'earning bread
and water, if not bread and flesh, anywhere between the
Atlantic and the Mississippi, by teaching Latin, Greek, or
English'. When Emerson encouraged him, Clough decided
to go, sailing from Liverpool for Boston on the *Canada*,
October 30 of the same year. This is a ship letter.

Meanwhile, in August Clough had been with Arnold in
Wales (M. A.'s *Letters*, i. 22), where they had talked of the
Poems of 1852, which appeared in October. 'The article' to
which Arnold here agrees is Clough's prospective review of
these poems. It finally appeared in the *North American Review*
for July, 1853 (vol. lxxvii, no. 160).]

Milford B.[oys] S.[chool] Oct^{ber} 28 [18]52

My dear Clough

I have got your note: Shairp I hope will come to me for
a day, and then he can bring the money.

As to that article. I am anxious to say that so long as I
am prosperous, nothing would please me more than for

you to make use of me, at any time, as if I were your brother.

And now what shall I say? First as to the poems. Write me from America concerning them, but do not read them in the hurry of this week. Keep them, as the Solitary did his Bible, for the silent deep.[1]

More and more I feel that the difference between a mature and a youthful age of the world compels the poetry of the former to use great plainness of speech as compared with that of the latter: and that Keats and Shelley were on a false track when they set themselves to reproduce the exuberance of expression, the charm, the richness of images, and the felicity, of the Elizabethan poets.[2] Yet critics cannot get to learn this, because the Elizabethan poets are our greatest, and our canons of poetry are founded on their works. They still think that the object of poetry is to produce exquisite bits and images—such as Shelley's *clouds shepherded by the slow unwilling wind*, and Keats passim: whereas modern poetry can only subsist by its *contents*: by becoming a complete magister vitae as the poetry of the ancients did: by including, as theirs did, religion with poetry, instead of existing as poetry only, and leaving religious wants to be supplied by the Christian religion, as a power existing independent of the poetical power. But the language, style and general proceedings of a poetry which has such an immense task to perform, must be very plain direct and severe: and it must not lose itself in parts and episodes and ornamental work, but must press forwards to the whole.

A new sheet will cut short my discourse: however, let us, as far as we can, continue to exchange our thoughts, as with all our differences we agree more with one another than with the rest of the world, I think. What do you say to a bi-monthly mail?

It was perhaps as well that the Rugby meeting was a Bacchic rout, for after all on those occasions there is nothing to be said.—God bless you wherever you go—with all my scepticism I can still say that. I shall go over and see Miss Smith from Hampton in December, and perhaps take Fanny Lucy with me. I am not very well or in very good

spirits, but I subsist:—what a difference there is between
reading in poetry and morals of the loss of youth, and ex-
periencing it! And after all there is so much to be done, if
one could but do it.—Goodbye again and again, my dear
Clough—
                                    your ever affectionate
                                            M. ARNOLD.

¹ See Wordsworth, *The Excursion*, III. 861–4.
² In his insistence upon the harm the Elizabethans have done as
models for modern poets, Arnold shows that the 'Preface to the Poems
of 1853' was already in his mind. And his conviction of poetry's
becoming a *magister vitae*, and including religion within it, is a striking
early statement of his continued feeling that literature, in the religious
transitions of the age, would increasingly serve mankind:
'The future of poetry is immense, because in poetry, where it is
worthy of its high destinies, our race, as time goes on, will find an ever
surer and surer stay. There is not a creed which is not shaken, not an
accredited dogma which is not shown to be questionable, not a received tradition which does not threaten to dissolve. Our religion has
materialised itself in the fact, in the supposed fact; it has attached its
emotion to the fact, and now the fact is failing it. But for poetry the
idea is everything; the rest is a world of illusion, of divine illusion.
Poetry attaches its emotion to the idea; the idea *is* the fact. The
strongest part of our religion to-day is its unconscious poetry.' ('The
Study of Poetry', *Essays in Criticism*, 2nd series, pp. 1–2.)

41

                          Battersea. Dec^ber 14th 1852
My dear Clough
   —I write to you from an evening sitting of the candidates
for certificates at the Training School here. It is a Church
of England place but such is my respectability that I am
admitted to their mysteries.
   I have no doubt that you will do well *socially* in the
U[nited] States: you are English, you are well introduced
—and you have personal merit—the object for you is to do
well *commercially*. Value the first only so far as it helps the
second. It would be a poor consolation for having not
established oneself at the end of a year and a half to be able
to say—I have got into the best American Society. If you

are to succeed there, you will begin at once, and will be the fashion as a tutor.

What sort of beings are the Yankees really? Better or worse in masses than they are individually? They me font l'effet of a nation not having on a wedding garment.[1] It is true that the well born, the well mannered, the highly cultivated—are called no longer, because they have shown such incapacity for administering the world: but it is too bad that when our Heavenly Father has whipped in there long ugly yellow rascallions from the highways and hedges they should not clean and polish themselves a little before taking the places of honour.

As for my poems they have weight, I think, but little or no charm

> What Poets feel not, when they make,
> A pleasure in creating,
> The world, in *its* turn, will not take
> Pleasure in contemplating.[2]

There is an oracular quatrain for you, terribly true. I feel now where my poems (this set) are all wrong, which I did not a year ago: but I doubt whether I shall ever have heat and radiance enough to pierce the clouds that are massed round me. Not in my little social sphere indeed, with you and Walrond: there I could crackle to my grave—but vis à vis of the world.—This volume is going off though: a nice notice of it was in the Guardian—and Froude will review it in the April Westminster, calling me by my name.[3] He is much pleased.—You must tell me what Emerson says. Make him look at it. *You* in your heart are saying *mollis et exspes*[4] over again. But woe was upon me if I analysed not my situation: and Werter[,] Réné[,] and such like[,] none of them analyse the modern situation in its true *blankness* and *barrenness*, and *unpoetrylessness*.

Now my dear Clough you were a good boy to write when you did, but you are not to write me scraps across the ὑγρὰ κέλευθα* of the Atlantic, or I shall dry up as a correspondent. But write me a nice long letter as if I was

* *Odyssey*, iii. 71, 177, &c.

an ἀνάλογον (at least) of Miss Blanche Smith—and then we will establish a regular bimonthly mail. God bless you. Flu and I shall go and see Miss Smith from Hampton.

ever yours affectionately

M. A.

[1] For Arnold on America, see pp. 48–9, 66, 70, 81, 130, 132, 133.

[2] The quatrain was placed in his collected *Poems* under the title of 'A Caution to Poets'. It is significant that he is reflecting upon his recent *Empedocles* and its failure to 'give joy' (see 'Preface to Poems of 1853', *Mixed Essays, &c.*, pp. 487–9).

[3] i.e. although Arnold's name was indicated only by an 'A' on the title-page. James Anthony Froude gave Arnold much encouragement through the years of his poetical apprenticeship. There are two hitherto unprinted manuscript letters from Froude to Clough, in which occur the following passages:

(March 6, 1849):—'I admire Matt—to a very great extent. Only I don't see what business he has to parade his calmness and lecture us on resignation when he has never known what a storm is, and doesn't know what he has to resign himself to—I think he only knows the shady side of nature out of books—Still I think his versifying and generally his aesthetic power is quite wonderful. . . . On the whole he shapes better than *you* I think—but you have marble to cut out and he has only clay. I do not know that I should say 'only'. There are some things like the Forsaken Merman that sound right out from the heart.' (Clough MSS.)

But again Froude writes:

(November 22, 1853):—Matt A's Sohrab & Rustum is to my taste *all* but 'perfect'—I think he has overdone the plainness of expression which he so much studies particularly in the beginning. And those repetitions of words (the word 'tent' comes half a dozen times in the first 18 lines, however justified by Homer's examples certainly strikes an English ear unpleasantly). I don't think he studies enough the effect to be produced by the *sound* of words. . . . But the essentials, the working up of the situation is faultlessly beautiful.' (Clough MSS.)

[4] The *mollis et exspes*, which Arnold imagines is Clough's verdict on his poems, is from Horace, *Epodes*, xvi. 37:

Mollis et exspes

Inominata perprimat cubilia.

Clough had in 1851 written Miss Smith: '*The Strayed Reveller* you won't like. It has had a great effect on me though,—it and its writer—but it is over I hope. I don't mean to let it have any more—Do you know what is meant by 'mollis et exspes' (in Horace)—that is my feeling about it more recently. I hardly know whether I should like you to read it, but as you fancy.' (Clough MSS.)

However, on his departure for America, when his sweetheart was low-spirited and discouraged, he advised her to read over 'Matt Arnold on Morality'.

42

[Long before his departure for America, Clough had formed
the notion that Arnold was growing somewhat cold toward
him. From Boston he has apparently written a frank account
of his feeling. This letter is Arnold's answer. It fully explains
itself and the situation out of which Clough's impression arose.]

My dear Clough   Edgbaston. February 12th, 1853

I received your letter ten days since—just as I was leaving
London—but I have since that time had too much to do to
attempt answering it, or indeed to attempt any thing else
that needed any thing of 'recueillement'. I do not like to
put off writing any longer, but to say the truth I do not feel
in the vein to write even now, nor do I feel certain that I
can write as I should wish. I am past thirty, and three
parts iced over—and my pen, it seems to me is even stiffer
and more cramped than my feeling.

But I will write historically, as I can write naturally in
no other way. I did not really think you had been hurt at
anything I did or left undone while we were together in
town: that is, I did not think any impression of hurt you
might have had for a moment, had lasted. I remember
your being annoyed once or twice, and that I was vexed
with myself: but at that time I was absorbed in my speculations and plans and agitations respecting Fanny Lucy, and
was as egoistic and anti-social as possible. People in the
condition in which I then was always are. I thought I had
said this and explained one or two pieces of apparent care-
lessness in this way: and that you had quite understood it.
So entirely indeed am I convinced that being in love
generally unfits a man for the society of his friends, that I
remember often smiling to myself at my own selfishness in
half compelling you several times to meet me in the last
few months before you left England, and thinking that it
was only I who could make such unreasonable demands or
find pleasure in meeting and being with a person, for the
mere sake of meeting and being with them, without re-
garding whether they would be absent and preoccupied or
not. I never, while we were both in London, had any
feeling towards you but one of attachment and affection: if

I did not enter into much explanation when you expressed annoyance, it was really because I thought the mention of my circumstances accounted for all and more than all that had annoyed you. I remember Walrond telling me you were vexed one day that on a return to town after a longish absence I let him stop in Gordon Square without me: I was then expecting to find a letter—or something of that sort—it all seems trivial now, but it was enough at the time to be the cause of heedlessness selfishness and heartlessness—in all directions but one—without number. It ought not to have been so perhaps—but it was so—and I quite thought you had understood that it was so.

There was one time indeed—shortly after you had published the Bothie—that I felt a strong disposition to intellectual seclusion, and to the barring out all influences that I felt troubled without advancing me: but I soon found that it was needless to secure myself against a danger from which my own weakness even more than my strength—my coldness and want of intellectual robustness—sufficiently exempted me—and besides your company and mode of being always had a charm and a salutary effect for me, and I could not have foregone these on a mere theory of intellectual dietetics.

In short, my dear Clough, I cannot say more than that I really have clung to you in spirit more than to any other man—and have never been seriously estranged from you at any time—for the estrangement I have just spoken of was merely a contemplated one and it never took place: I remember saying something about it to you at the time— and your answer, which struck me for the genuineness and faith it exhibited as compared with my own—not want of faith exactly—but invincible languor of spirit, and fickleness and insincerity even in the gravest matters. All this is dreary work—and I cannot go on with it now: but tomorrow night I will try again—for I have one or two things more to say. Goodnight now.—

Sunday, 6 P.M.

I will not look at what I wrote last night—one endeavours to write deliberately out what is in one's mind, without any

veils of flippancy levity metaphor or demi-mot, and one
succeeds only in putting upon the paper a string of dreary
dead sentences that correspond to nothing in one's inmost
heart or mind, and only represent themselves. It was your
own fault partly for forcing me to it. I will not go on with
it: only remember, *pray* remember that I am and always
shall be, whatever I do or say, powerfully attracted towards
you, and vitally connected with you: this I am sure of: the
period of my developement (God forgive me the d—d expression!) coincides with that of my friendship with you so
exactly that I am for ever linked with you by intellectual
bonds—the strongest of all: more than you are with me: for
your developement was really over before you knew me,
and you had properly speaking come to your *assiette* for
life. You ask me in what I think or have thought you going
wrong: in this: that you would never take your assiette as
something determined final and unchangeable for you and
proceed to work away on the basis of that: but were always
poking and patching and cobbling at the assiette itself—
could never finally, as it seemed—'resolve to be thyself' [1]—
but were looking for this and that experience, and doubting
whether you ought not to adopt this or that mode of being
of persons qui ne vous valaient pas because it might possibly
be nearer the truth than your own: you had no reason for
thinking it *was*, but it *might* be—and so you would try to
adapt yourself to it. You have I am convinced lost infinite
time in this way: it is what I call your morbid conscien-
tiousness—you are the most conscientious man I ever
knew: but on some lines morbidly so, and it spoils your
action.

There—but now we will have done with this: we are
each very near to the other—write and tell me that you feel
this: as to my behaviour in London I have told you the
simple truth: it is I fear too simple than that (excuse the
idiom) you with your raffinements should believe and
appreciate it.

There is a power of truth in your letter and in what you
say about America and this country: yes—*congestion of the
brain* is what we suffer from—I always feel it and say it—
and cry for air like my own Empedocles. But this letter

shall be what it is. I have a number of things I want to talk to you about—they shall wait till I have heard again from you. Pardon me, but we *will* exchange intellectual aperçus—we shall both be the better for it. Only let us pray all the time—God keep us both from aridity! *Arid*—that is what the times are.—Write soon and tell me you are well—I was sure you were not well. God bless you. Flu sends her kindest remembrances. ever yours

M. A.

We called the other day at Combe Hurst[2] but found vacuas sedes et inania arcana. But we shall meet in town. What does Emerson say to my poems—or is he gone crazy as Miss Martineau says. But this is probably one of her d——d lies.[3] Once more fare*well*, in every sense.

[1]   *Resolve to be thyself*; and know that he,
              Who finds himself, loses his misery!
is the conclusion of Arnold's *Self-Dependence*.

[2] The home of Miss Blanche Smith.

[3] Harriet Martineau (1802–76), the writer, was a neighbour of the Arnold family at Fox How. Arnold's opinions of her are varied from time to time. He was glad enough to have a chance to 'speak of her with respect' in his 'Haworth Churchyard' (see *Letters*, i. 50–1): 'I cannot but praise a person whose one effort seems to have been to deal perfectly honestly with herself, although for the speculations into which this effort has led her I have not the slightest sympathy.' In 1869, he recalls, 'Miss Martineau has always been a good friend to me' (*Letters* ii. 6). But in 1877 he informs an acquaintance, 'I had forgotten the poem about Charlotte Brontë and Harriet Martineau, but I will look it up. I think there were things not bad in it, but I do not want to overpraise a personage so antipathetic to me as H. M. My first impression of her is, in spite of her undeniable talent, energy, and merit—what an unpleasant life and unpleasant nature!' (*Letters*, ii. 158).

For the reference to Emerson, see the next letter, p. 132.

43

23. Grosvenor St. West [London]
Grosvenor Place
March 21 [18]53.

My dear Clough

I got your letter at Halstead in Essex on Friday evening last. This is the thinnest paper I can lay my hand upon: would that I could but write upon it. We will not discuss

what is past any more: as to the Italian poem,¹ if I forbore
to comment it was that I had nothing special to say—what
is to be said when a thing does not suit you—suiting and
not suiting is a subjective affair and only time determines,
by the colour a thing takes with years, whether it *ought* to
have suited or no.

I am glad to hear a good account of Emerson's health—
I thought his insanity was one of Miss Martineau's terrific
lies: sane he certainly is, though somewhat incolore as the
French say—very thin and ineffectual, and self-defensive
only. Tell me when you can something about his life and
manner of going on—and his standing in the Boston world.²

Margaret Fuller³—what do you think of her? I have
given, after some hesitation, half a guinea for the three
volumes concerning her—partly moved by the low price
partly by interest about that partly brazen female. I incline to think that the meeting with her would have made
me return all the contents of my spiritual stomach but
through the screen of a book I willingly look at her and
allow her her exquisite intelligence and fineness of aperçus.
But my G—d what rot did she and the other female dogs
of Boston talk about the Greek mythology! The absence of
men of any culture in America, where everybody knows
that the Earth is an oblate speroid and nobody knows anything worth knowing, must have made her run riot so
wildly, and for many years made her insufferable.

Miss Bronte⁴ has written a hideous undelightful con-
vulsed constricted novel—what does Thackeray say to it.
It is one of the most utterly disagreeable books I ever read
—and having seen her makes it more so. She is so entirely
—what Margaret Fuller was partially—a fire without
aliment—one of the most distressing barren sights one can
witness. Religion or devotion or whatever it is to be called
may be impossible for such people now: but they have at
any rate not found a substitute for it and it was better for
the world when they comforted themselves with it.

Thackeray's Esmond you know everyone here calls a
failure—but I do not think so. it is one of the most readable
books I ever met—and Thackeray is certainly a first rate
journeyman though not a great artist:—It gives you an

insight into the *heaven born* character of Waverley and Indiana and such like when you read the undeniably powerful but most un-heaven-born productions of the present people—Thackeray—the woman Stowe etc. The woman Stowe[5] by her picture must be a Gorgon—I can quite believe all you tell me of her—a strong Dissenter-religious middle-class person—she will never go far, I think.

Look at Alexander Smith's poems[6] which some people speak of and let me know what you think of them. The article on Wordsworth, I hear, is Lockhart's,[7] very just though cold. Perhaps it does not sufficiently praise his *diction*: his *manner* was often bad, but his diction scarcely ever—and beyond Moore's etc.—constantly.

Goodnight—no more paper.

Read some articles of Ampère's in the Revue des 2 Mondes on America:[8] what he says is so cool clear désabusé and true that it will do you good in the atmosphere of inflation exaggeration and intoxication in which you live.

We will yet see the young lady—though not soon, I fear. I am frightfully worked at present. I read Homer and toujours Homer.[9]   ever yours

                                      M. A.

Susy[10] is going to be married to John Cropper—second son of the principal Liverpool Cropper.

[1] Clough's *Amours de Voyage*. Although the poem was a product of his visit to Rome in 1849, he kept it by him for nine years. James Russell Lowell finally bought it for the *Atlantic Monthly*, where it ran February–May 1858.

[2] Arnold's considered judgement on Emerson is contained in his lecture of 1883, where he denies him high rank as a poet, a prose writer, or a philosopher, but praises him as a 'friend and aider of all who would live in the spirit' (*Discourses in America*, pp. 138 ff.).

[3] The estimate of Margaret Fuller (1810–50) is not wholly distinguished by 'urbanity' and 'proportion'; but Arnold also properly sets forth her merits. About this same time he wrote his mother, 'I have been reading Margaret Fuller, and again have been struck with her sincere striving to be good and helpful. Her address to the poor women in the Penitentiary is really beautiful. "Cultivate the spirit of prayer. I do not mean agitation and excitement, but a deep desire for truth, purity, and goodness, and you will daily learn how near He is to every one of us." Nothing can be better than that' (*Letters*, i. 36).

[4] Charlotte Brontë also takes her place in this dream of distressing women. *Villette* is disagreeable because, as he says to his sister, 'the

writer's mind contains nothing but hunger, rebellion, and rage, and therefore that is all she can, in fact, put into her book. No fine writing can hide this thoroughly, and it will be fatal to her in the long run' (*Letters*, i. 34).

⁵ One comes with some surprise upon *Uncle Tom's Cabin* in Arnold's library. The novel had been commended by W. E. Forster, Arnold's brother-in-law, in the *Westminster Review* for January 1853. The article was unsigned, but the secret of its authorship was soon known among the abolitionists in America (Sir Wemyss Reid, *Life of W. E. Forster*, Chapman & Hall, London, 1888, i. 288 ff.).

⁶ The poems of Alexander Smith (1830–67) were discussed by Clough in the same article in the *North American Review* in which he considered Arnold's work.

⁷ See *The Quarterly Review*, xcii. (March 1853) pp. 182–236. The statement that Wordsworth's diction is scarcely ever bad is contradicted, of course, in 'A French Critic on Milton'. There Arnold calls to our mind the perpetual level of Milton by considering 'the ever-recurring failure, both in rhythm and in diction, which we find in the so-called Miltonic blank verse of Thomson, Cowper, Wordsworth. What leagues of lumbering movement! what desperate endeavours, as in Wordsworth's

And at the Hoop alighted, famous inn'.

(See *Mixed Essays, &c.*, p. 200.)

⁸ Ampère's serial account of his *Promenade en Amérique* appeared in eight instalments in the *Revue des Deux Mondes* during the first half of the year 1853. Ampère finds that the fixed idea of Americans is 'l'occupation constante et la glorification perpétuelle de la patrie—la conviction de la supériorité de leur pays est au fond de tout ce qu'ils disent' (*R. des Deux Mondes*, xxiii⁰ année, seconde série de la nouvelle période, tome premier, January 1, 1853, p. 7).

⁹ Arnold's note-books reveal that he was, indeed, reading Homer, and 'toujours Homer'. That and Milton were daily preparation for *Sohrab and Rustum*, which he was then composing.

¹⁰ Susan Arnold was a younger sister.

44

[This letter recurs apparently to the misunderstanding aired in Letter 42.

While Arnold was busy on *Sohrab and Rustum*, Clough began in America his revision of what is known as Dryden's translation of Plutarch's *Lives*, a task he thoroughly enjoyed.]

My dear Clough   London. May 1, 1853

I do not know that the tone of your letters exactly facilitates correspondence—however, let it be as you will. I for my part think that what Curran¹ said of the constitution of the state holds true of individual moral constitutions: it does not do to lay bare their foundations too constantly. It is very true I am not myself in writing—but it is of no use reproaching me with it, since so it must be.

I do not think we did each other harm at Oxford. I look back to that time with pleasure. All activity to which the conscience does not give its consent is mere *philistercy*, and it is always a good thing to have been preserved from this. I catch myself desiring now at times political life, and this and that; and I say to myself—you do not desire these things because you are really adapted to them, and therefore the desire for them is merely contemptible—and it is so. I am nothing and very probably never shall be anything— but there are characters which are truest to themselves by never being anything, when circumstances do not suit. If you had never met me, I do not think you would have been the happier or the wiser on that account: though I do not think I have increased your stock of happiness. You have, however, on the whole, added to mine. You do not tell me what you are doing; Mrs. Lingen told me last night you had six pupils: she is a great friend you know of *your* friend's: we talked a great deal about you—not that I like her (Mrs. Lingen) much. Your friend has been to see Fanny Lucy— but I was from home: I shall manage to see her some day. You will come all right, I think, when you are once married.

If you have been looking over North's Plutarch lately you are probably right about it—but I cannot help thinking (I am going on with this Tuesday night May 3rd) that there is a freshness in his style and language which is like a new world to one—it produces the same effect on me as Cotton's Montaigne does:—if North could be read *safely*, without one's continually suspecting an error, and in a handy volume, I think he would be delightful reading. You are quite right to incorporate Long.[2] I should much like to see what you have done. Stick to literature—it is the great comforter after all. I should like to read an article of your's on me—I should read it with a curious feeling—my version of Tristram and Iseult comes from an article in the Revue de Paris, on Fauriel,[3] I think: the story of Merlin is imported from the Morte d'Arthur. If I republish that poem I shall try to make it more intelligible: I wish I had you with me to put marks against the places where something is wanted. The whole affair is by no means thoroughly successful.

I have just got through a thing⁴ which pleases me better than anything I have yet done—but it is pain and grief composing with such interruptions as I have: however in this case the material was a thoroughly good one, and what a thing is this! and how little do young writers feel what a thing it is—how it is *everything*.

I feel immensely—more and more clearly—what I *want* —what I have (I believe) lost and choked by my treatment of myself and the studies to which I have addicted myself. But what ought I to have done in preference to what I have done? there is the question.

As to Alexander Smith I have not read him—I shrink from what is so intensely immature—but I think the extracts I have seen most remarkable—and I think at the same time that he will not go far. I have not room or time for my reasons—but I think so. This kind does not go far: it dies like Keats or loses itself like Browning.

You know (or you do not know) that Froude, who is one of the very few people who much liked my last vein,* or to be other than the black villain my Maker made me.⁵ Tell me about yourself—and above all do not dream of my using you as food for speculation: that is simply a morbid suspicion: I like to hear all about you because I am fond of you.

Good bye again—
            Your incorrigible and affectionate
                                                M. A.

My father's journals are out—they are a mere bookseller's

---

* As it stands, this passage is not intelligible. The confusion in the text arises after a crossment (in the preceding paragraph Arnold says he has left only little 'room or time') back to the first sheet. There he apparently forgets his original construction. I suggest as an approximation to the intended reading: 'You know (or you do not know) that Froude is one of the very few people who much liked my last vein, or thought me to be other than the black villain my maker made me.'

catchpenny, in my judgment:[6] but they are a convenient size—but there is nothing new in them.

[1] Arnold has in mind Curran's discussion of the British constitution at the trial of Archibald Rowan: 'This is a kind of subject which I feel myself overawed when I approach. There are certain fundamental principles which nothing but necessity should expose to a public examination; they are pillars, the depth of whose foundation you cannot explore without endangering their strength'. (*Speeches of John Philpot Curran*, New York, 1811, pp. 68–9.)

[2] For Arnold's praise of Long as a translator, see 'Marcus Aurelius', *Essays in Criticism*, 1st series, pp. 349 ff.: 'In his notes on Plutarch's Roman Lives he deals with the modern epoch of Caesar and Cicero, not as food for schoolboys, but as food for men, and men engaged in the current of contemporary life and action.'

[3] The source of *Tristram and Iseult*, as we here learn for the first time, is Théodore de la Villemarqué's articles in the *Revue de Paris* on *Les Poèmes Gallois et les romans de la Table Ronde*, which treat of Fauriel's work and give the story of Tristram and Iseult, principally in the first article. (See *Revue de Paris*, series 3, vol. xxxiv, 1841, pp. 266–82, 335–48.) Arnold says his account of Merlin and Vivien came from Malory, but there are two articles which may have helped him. They are: Villemarqué's *Visite au tombeau de Merlin* in *Revue de Paris*, 2nd series, vol. xli, 1837, pp. 45–62; and Louandre's *L'Enchanteur Merlin* (ibid., 3rd series, vol. xvi, 1840, pp. 109–22).

Observe (Letter 47) that the extract from Dunlop's *History of Fiction* was not prefaced to the poem until after the 1853 edition was planned, and then at Froude's suggestion.

[4] *Sohrab and Rustum*.

[5] For Froude's interest in Arnold, see p. 140.

[6] Only a small portion of Dr. Arnold's travel diaries was printed. The complete MS. is now the property of Mrs. Florence Vere O'Brien.

45

[In July 1853 Clough returned from America to accept a post in the Education Office. This position made it possible for him to marry on June 12 of the following year. His new duties began on July 25. After consulting Arnold's MS. journals, which show him at Bangor on Wednesday, July 27, I select that as the likely date of the letter. Observe his phrase: 'Let me know how you start.' Arnold had previously welcomed Clough home in London.]

Penrhyn Arms. Bangor.

My dear Clough   Wednesday night. [July 27, 1853]

I sincerely wish you were here. To be amongst Tals and Pens and Llans makes my thoughts turn to you at once—

ıld so like being here, I know.—I wonder if a
erved at Colwyn today was your Aunt's.
ıth great pleasure last night in bed your article
Theories.[1] Much of it was truly noble, and well
3ut you have yet to learn a sort of literary economy,
ʷ⸗ ⸗bids to *gaspiller* your treasures. Choose, as far as
you can, *adequate subjects*, and put your mark upon them.
But I have more and more respect for your literary ability,
and wholesome abundance, so unlike the strangled poverty
stricken driblets of some of us.

Now you are again in London, cultivate all sorts of ac-
quaintances, your Lewises[2] and all. It is one of your best
circumstances that you get on with these men and that
they like you. And their acquaintance is almost indispensable for a practical acquaintance with these times.

I said nothing while we were together about the subject
of your letters—or many of them—because I thought there
was no need so to do. We will leave the past to itself—for
the present I can sincerely say that I never felt more strongly
than now—or so strongly—how close I am to you—and,
in my own feeling, to you alone.

Let me know how you start. I am inclined to think you
will toss off the work very easily. £300 a year, got without
grimacing or false pretences, is something certainly which
deserves respect, and attention before one rejects it.

You will laugh if I tell you I am deplorably ennuyé. I
seem to myself to have lost all ressort—

> For whom each year we see
> Breeds new beginnings, disappointments new[3]—

One gets tired at last of one's own clasticity.
Write to me at the Beaumaris Post office.

ever yours affectionately
M. A.

---

[1] For extracts from a review of 'a work entitled "Considerations on
Some Recent Social Theories"', cf. Clough's *Prose Remains*, pp. 405 ff.
[2] Sir George Cornewall Lewis (1806–63), formerly financial secretary at the Treasury, editor of the *Edinburgh Review* from December
1852 to February 28, 1855.
[3] Quoted from *The Scholar Gipsy*, stanza 18, lines 6–7.

46
Well my dear Clough you should have been with me tonight to see the sunset of our first fine day over the great
Carnarvonshire promontory. What an outline is that! The
most accurate lurid Mediterranean thing in these islands, eh?

  If you knew the refreshment it was to me to think of you
in London again. Froude expressed himself warmly on
this head yesterday. He dined with us at Beddgelert (Flu
and me) as we passed through yesterday. I stay with him
for two days a fortnight hence—perhaps ascend Snowdon
by night with him. He is *softened* more than I can tell you,
but I think in baddish spirits. Kingsley has been staying
with him. His poem is in hexameters, and on *Perseus and
Andromeda*. Eh? Froude says much of it is very good. Now
I think, a priori, the man is too *coarse a workman* for poetry.

  I have written out my Sohrab and Rustum, and like it less.
—Composition, in the painter's sense—that is the devil. And,
when one thinks of it, our painters cannot *compose* though
they can show great genius—so too in poetry is it not to be
expected that in this same article of *composition* the awkward
incorrect Northern nature should shew itself? though we
may have feeling—fire—eloquence—as much as our betters.

  I am trying to re-read Valentine [1]—but stick—except in
the scenery bits. I am beginning the Tempest. How ill he
often writes! but how often too how incomparably! [2]

  Write to me at Beaumaris my dear. Perhaps you have:
I have been away these three days.

  See that the Minutes for last year are sent to the *Holyhead*
and *Duffryn* schools. Tell me about your work.
                        your affectionate
                             M. A.
Read the details [3] about poor Keats at the end of Haydon's
first and the beginning of his second vol. Haydon himself
is a false *butcher*—revolting.

[1] George Sand's novel.
  [2] For Arnold's ideas on poetry, see pp. 39 et seq.; for his criticism of
Shakespeare, pp. 45–6, 65, 143, 146.
  [3] The 'details' are used by Arnold in his essay on Keats (*Essays in
Criticism*, 2nd series, pp. 100–2).

47

[Fox How, his mother's home in Ambleside, was the scene of Arnold's vacations from the schools. Here he fished, and did much of his best reading and writing each year.

Clough has now fully entered on his work at the Education Office.]

Fox How. August 25th [1853]

My dear Clough

Here I am at last nearly stupified by 8 months inspecting. However I am in better health than usual thanks to knocking about in open cars in Wales. Several of the Welsh Managers are complaining that they have not got the last volumes of Minutes—will you just ask how this is.

I should like you to see Froude[1]—quantum mutatus! He goes to church, has family prayers—says the Nemesis ought never to have been published etc. etc.—his friends say that he is altogether changed and re-entered within the giron de l'Eglise—at any rate within the giron de la religion chrétienne: but I do not see the matter in this light and think that he conforms in the same sense in which Spinoza advised his mother to conform—and having purified his moral being, all that was mere fume and vanity and love of notoriety and opposition in his proceedings he has abandoned and regrets. This is my view. He is getting more and more literary, and vise au solide instead of beating the air. May we all follow his example!

Did I tell you he dislikes all Hexameters. I repeated to him some I thought my best—he said he thought they were as good as any, but not the thing.

William Forster who has been very ill is here. They think here that your article on me[2] is obscure and peu favorable—but I do not myself think either of these things. I told you Froude says he can certainly review me in January.

He recommends prefacing Tristram and Iseult with an extract from Dunlop's Hist. of fiction to tell the story, in preference to telling it in my own words: thus also to preface Mycerinus with a literal translation of the passage of Herodotus which concerns him. I think this is good advice.

He rather discounsels from a preface, but I shall try my
hand at it, at any rate, I think. I thought of a division of
the poems according to their character and subject, into
Antiquity—Middle Age—and Temps Moderne—but this
also he dissuades from. What do you think?
Write me a good long letter and not a scrubby scrap.
Tell me how you get on.

ever yours

M. A.

¹ Froude had published in 1849 his *Nemesis of Faith*, which cost him
his fellowship. The Senior Tutor of Exeter in the midst of a lecture
had burnt the book in the College Hall. (See Herbert Paul, *The Life
of Froude*, New York, 1906.) The hexameters Arnold showed Froude
were doubtless attempts at translating the *Iliad*. We can be deeply
grateful that, while he took so much of Froude's counsel, Arnold was
not dissuaded from the Preface to the Poems of 1853, which is in some
respects his most important critical utterance.

² In his review of Arnold's first two volumes of poems and of other
English verse (see *North American Review*, vol. lxxvii, No. 160, July,
1853, pp. 1–30) Clough had been on the whole favourable. He did
make certain strictures upon obscurities in *Tristram and Iseult*, upon
the poet's tendency to assign too high a place to 'what we call Nature',
and upon his too great confinement within 'the dismal cycle of his
rehabilitated Hindoo-Greek theosophy'.

In the two following quotations one learns rather well what Clough
thought of Arnold at the time:

'[The poems] are, it would seem, the productions of a scholar and a
gentleman; a man who has received a refined education, seen refined
"society", and been more, we dare say, in the world, which is called
the world, than in all likelihood has a Glasgow mechanic [i.e. Alexander Smith]. More refined, therefore, and more highly educated sensi-
bilities—too delicate, are they, for common service?—a calmer judgment also, a more poised and steady intellect, the *siccum lumen* of the
soul; a finer and rarer aim perhaps, and certainly a keener sense of
difficulty, in life;—these are the characteristics of him whom we are to
call "A."'

And later in the review: 'Meantime, it is one promising point in our
author of the initial, that his second is certainly on the whole an improvement upon his first volume. There is less obvious study of effect;
upon the whole, a plainer and simpler and less factitious manner and
method of treatment. This, he may be sure, is the only safe course.
Not by turning and twisting his eyes, in the hope of seeing things as
Homer, Sophocles, Virgil, or Milton saw them; but by seeing them,
by accepting them as he sees them, and faithfully depicting accord-
ingly, will he attain the object he desires.'

141

48

Fox How. September 6th [1853]

My dear Clough

When more than one Candidate is examined you shall have all the papers: but it continually happens that for one vacancy only one Candidate is examined, and it would not do to insist upon having a spare candidate to fall back upon *in case* the successful one afterwards miscarried, as a boy who is examined is always disappointed if he is not taken.

Blackett is here, and goes on Thursday. I have sent him this evening to a ball with my sisters—it is a great pleasure having him here. Conington and Goldwin Smith are reading at Grasmere and dine with us tomorrow. Goldwin Smith has the funereal solemnity of an undertaker: I suppose he caught it from Conington. They are working hard at an edition of Virgil.[1]

If you have opportunity look at an article on India in *August's* Fraser.[2] It is by my brother Willy, but do not mention this: It is poor in ideas, but see if you do not think the style very vigorous.

London must be getting awful, and I suppose you have no chance of leaving it. Sandford's[3] return will be a godsend—he is a far better fellow than Lingen and has real geniality—remember me to him particularly. Lingen I think a bore.[4]

As to conformity I only recommend it in so far as it frees us from the unnatural and unhealthy attitude of contradiction and opposition—the *Qual der Negation* as Goethe calls it. Only positive convictions and feeling are worth anything—and the glow of these one can never feel so long as one is pugnacious and out of temper. This is my firm belief.

I do not believe that the Reformation caused the Elizabethan literature—but that both sprang out of the active animated condition of the human spirit in Europe at that time. After the fall of the Roman Empire the barbarians powerfully turned up the soil of Europe—and after a little time when the violent ploughing was over and things had settled a little, a vigorous crop of new ideas was the result. Italy bore the first crop—but the soil having been before much exhausted soon left bearing. The virgin soils of Germany and England went on longer—but they too are I think beginning to fail. I think there never yet has been a perfect literature or a perfect art because the energetic nations spoil them by their illusions and their want of taste—and the nations who lose their illusions lose also their energy and creative power. Certainly Goethe had all the *negative* recommendations for a perfect artist but he wanted the *positive*—Shakespeare had the positive and wanted the negative. The Iliad and what I know of Raphael's works seem to me to be in a juster measure and a happier vein than anything else.

If one loved what was beautiful and interesting in itself *passionately* enough, one would produce what was excellent without troubling oneself with religious dogmas at all. As it is, we are *warm* only when dealing with these last—and what is frigid is always bad. I would have others—most others stick to the old religious dogmas because I sincerely feel that this *warmth* is the great blessing, and this frigidity the great curse—and on the old religious road they have still the best chance of getting the one and avoiding the other.[5]

ever yours
M. A.

Republish at Boston by all means.

[1] The work was begun together, but Smith was forced to drop his part of the task before it was well under way.

[2] William Delafield Arnold's article entitled *What Is the Indian Question?*, appeared in *Fraser's Magazine*, xlviii (1853), pp. 234–48.

[3] Francis Richard John Sandford (1824–93), whom Arnold had known at Balliol, entered the Education Office in 1848. He was made a baron in 1891.

[4] Arnold's irritation is not very deep. William Ralph Lingen (1819–1905) had been a fellow at Balliol while Arnold was there. He became Education Secretary in 1849, to do a valuable and conscientious work. His formal and exacting standards, however, at times gained the momentary dislike of his associates. Arnold remembered him, on other occasions, as his old Oxford tutor and 'a genius of good counsel'. (See *Letters*, i. 16 and ii. 29–30.) Mr. Humphry Ward records,

moreover, Arnold's estimate of Lingen as 'one of the best and most faithful public servants' (*Reign of Queen Victoria*, ii. 258).

⁵ The ideas Arnold raises here are, for the most part, treated in the Introduction. His praise of religious warmth prepares us for his later conception of 'morality touched by emotion' and the whole of his preface to *Literature and Dogma*.

49

[See date at end]

My dear Clough

I am greatly a debtor both to you and to Poste¹ for your trouble, although you have not found my passage. But never mind—I have boldly quoted it from memory—it consists only of a single line.

Forgive my scold the other day—when one is trying to emerge to hard land it is irritating to find your friend not only persisting in 'weltering to the parching wind' himself, but doing his best to pull you back into the Sea also.

The Preface² is done—there is a certain *Geist* in it I think, but it is far less *precise* than I had intended. How difficult it is to write prose: and why? because of the *articulations of the discourse*: one leaps these over in Poetry—places one thought cheek by jowl with another without introducing them and leaves them—but in prose this will not do. It is of course not right in poetry either—but we all do it: you meant something of this in your expression about *sequence* in that article,³ which struck me as a lovely aperçu when I read it.

I am here for 6 weeks, busy enough—I really think the new volume will do—but time will shew.

Imagine a claim from Oriel for £30 for caution money. What on earth is to be done.

ever yours affectionately

Pray thank Poste again for me.   M. ARNOLD.—
Derby October 10ᵗʰ [1853]

¹ Edward Poste, barrister, had known Arnold at Oriel.
² The Preface to the Poems of 1853.
³ In his article in the *North American Review* Clough had criticized some portions of Alexander Smith's poems for lacking ' that happy, unimpeded sequence which is the charm of really good writers' [*N. A. R.*, vol. lxxvii, No. 160 (1853), p. 26].

50

My dear Clough   Derby. Nov^{ber} 25/53.

Just read through Tennyson's Morte d'Arthur and
Sohrab and Rustum one after the other, and you will see
the difference in the *tissue* of the style of the two poems, and
in its *movement*. I think the likeness, where there is likeness,
(except in the two last lines which I own are a regular slip [1])
proceeds from our both having imitated Homer. But never
mind—you are a dear soul. I am in great hopes you will
one day like the poem—really like it. There is no one to
whose aperçus I attach the value I do to yours—but I
think you are sometimes—with regard to *me* especially—
a little cross and wilful.

I send your two letters [2]—not that you may see the praise
of me in them (and I can sincerely say that praise of *myself*
—talking about imagination—genius and so on—does not
give me, at heart, the slightest flutter of pleasure—seeing
people interested in what I have made, does—) but that
you may see how heartily two very different people seem
to have taken to Sohrab and Rustum. This is something,
at any rate. Hill's criticism is always delicate and good—
and his style in prose has something of the beauty of his
father in law's.[3] How well all the third page is written.

Return me the letters—write a line to P. O. Lincoln. I
am worked to death. God bless you. ever yours   M. A.

[1] The slip by which he has imitated Tennyson, in part, refers,
I think, to the resemblance of the last two lines of *Sohrab and Rustum*
to the following lines (242-3) of *Morte d'Arthur*:
> And on a sudden lo! the level lake,
> And the long glories of the winter moon.

[2] Letters received by Arnold upon the publication of the *Poems* of
1853, in which *Sohrab and Rustum* had just appeared.

[3] Herbert Hill, a former tutor of both Matthew and Tom Arnold,
had married Bertha, daughter of Robert Southey.

51

My dear Clough   Coleby—November 30th [1853]

I think 'if indeed this one desire rules all' [1]—*is* rather
Tennysonian—at any rate it is not good.

The resemblance in the other passage I cannot for the life of me see.

I think the poem[2] has, if not the *rapidity*, at least the *fluidity* of Homer: and that it is in this respect that it is un-Tennysonian: and that it is a sense of this which makes Froude and Blackett say it is a step in advance of Tennyson in this strain.

A thousand things make one compose or not compose: composition seems to keep alive in me a *cheerfulness*—a sort of Tuchtigkeit, or natural soundness and valiancy, which I think the present age is fast losing—this is why I like it.

I am glad you like the Gipsy Scholar—but what does it *do* for you? Homer *animates*—Shakespeare *animates*—in its poor way I think Sohrab and Rustum *animates*—the Gipsy Scholar at best awakens a pleasing melancholy.[3] But this is not what we want.

> The complaining millions of men
> Darken in labour and pain—[4]

what they want is something to *animate* and *ennoble* them— not merely to add zest to their melancholy or grace to their dreams.—I believe a feeling of this kind is the basis of my nature—and of my poetics.

You certainly do not seem to me sufficiently to desire and earnestly strive towards—assured knowledge—activity— happiness. You are too content to *fluctuate*—to be ever learning, never coming to the knowledge of the truth. This is why, with you, I feel it necessary to stiffen myself— and hold fast my rudder.

My poems, however, viewed *absolutely*, are certainly little or nothing.

I shall be in town on Friday night I hope. I will then speak to you about Caroline Hall, the Derby P.T.

ever yours affectionately
M. ARNOLD.—

[1] The 74th line of *Sohrab and Rustum*, which was changed in 1854 to read:
'But, if this one desire indeed rules all'
from its original form:
'But if indeed this one desire rules all'.
It is clear that Arnold associates Tennyson with a light, too musical

cadence, far too gentle and regular for the sterner Homeric tone intended for *Sohrab*.

² *Sohrab and Rustum.*

³ The unfavourable criticism Arnold makes of 'The Scholar Gipsy' is, of course, important. But it must be taken only *relatively* here. Arnold endeavours constantly to set Clough against sentiments that were too dangerously congenial to him anyhow.

⁴ Quoted from Arnold's *The Youth of Nature*, 51–2.

52

[With both Arnold and Clough centred in London, there are few letters for the later years. The present one shows how 'the dance of death in the elementary schools' interrupted work in poetry.

On June 12, 1854, Clough had married Miss Blanche Smith, and in a house near Regent's Park begun the quiet family life that lasted for seven years. During this period three children were born, the first of whom died in infancy. His work of translating Plutarch relieved somewhat the routine of the Education Office. He was also deeply concerned over the Crimean War, and the part played in it by Florence Nightingale, his wife's cousin. The constant assistance he later rendered her forms almost a separate chapter in the closing years of his life.]

Brighton. August 2, 1855

My dear Clough

This day I send in *Deal Wes*ⁿ (an August case)—will you kindly take it promptly as Harris the master has received one of the appointments to New S. Walcs and will sail very shortly?

Will you also see why Annie Hinchley, Mistress of the Dunmon B. S. has not had her certificate sent to her?

I wish you would write me a long letter. From the extracts I have seen from Maud,¹ he seems in his old age to be coming to your manner in the Bothie and the Roman poem. That manner, as you know, I do not like: but certainly, if it is to be used, you use it with far more freedom vigour and abundance than he does—Altogether I think this volume a lamentable production, and like so much of our literature thoroughly and intensely *provincial*, not European.

With the usual prayer that no fine spirits may be so

drenched in the daily cares of life as finally to become imbruted, I remain,

Your friend to command

M. A.

¹ Tennyson's *Maud, and Other Poems* had just appeared. There were, however, considerable additions made to the title poem the following year.

In December 1857 Arnold gave Clough a copy of *Merope*, his verse tragedy. He inscribes the following significant quotation from Goethe:

'Mit wahrhaft Gleichgesinnten kann man sich auf die Länge entzweien, man findet sich immer wieder nicht zusammen; mit eigentlich Widergesinnten versucht man umsonst Einigkeit zu halten, es bricht immer wieder einmal auseinander.'*

In January 1859 he inscribed also upon a presentation copy of Virgil: 'To A. H. C. Eheu! fugaces'.

53

[In order to make a study of European education, Arnold made a long visit to the Continent in 1859. In August he came back to England for a short interval.

His pamphlet, *England and the Italian Question*, had just been published. It argued for the natural independence of Italy, but also represented Louis Napoleon's intervention there as disinterested. On August 13, Arnold wrote to his sister, 'You and Clough are, I believe, the two people I in my heart care most to please by what I write. Clough (for a wonder) is this time satisfied, even delighted, "with one or two insignificant exceptions", he says.']

1, Wellesley Terrace, Dover—

August 11ᵗʰ, 1859.

My dear old soul. I find that, au fond, when I compose anything, I care more, still, for your opinion than that of any one else about it—so you may imagine what pleasure

* Arnold's slightly selective version of Goethe, 'Maximen und Reflexionen', section IX, number 582, p. 223. *Werke*, vol. 24, Meyers Klassiker-Ausgaben. 'With truly like-minded people one cannot in the long run be at outs, one finds oneself always eventually together again; with people of really opposite views a man tries in vain to come to any unity; it is continually so breaking apart.'

your note, received this morning, gave me. It had been lying in Chester Square, and was forwarded by a chance opportunity. I had supposed that you thought me still abroad. Indeed I am only here for a few days, to get some Kent schools done, and few know my address.

I use *reason* from a way of thinking I have about the ancient and modern or ante Christian and post Christian worlds, which I am not sure that you sympathise in, which I am developing in my lectures, and which it would be tedious to talk about here.[1]

The correction about the Prussian army is most important.[2] I have no knowledge of Prussia from personal experience—I was astonished at what I heard from French officers about their army—finding myself one day at dinner, in Paris, by a Prussian diplomate, I questioned him closely on the subject—not making any distinction, certainly between officers and men, but talking of l'armée Prussienne. I could hardly believe that they had not even picked troops, guards, or a household brigade, who served for longer than 3 years. He assured me they had not, however, and himself thought it a cause of weakness for the Prussian army, though not to the same extent that the French do. The French lay the most astonishing stress on *old soldiers* and having *seen service*: it would astonish you to find how they value the Crimean training for their men, and they say it is worth our while to have a perpetual Indian mutiny for the good it does our troops. If you assure me that you *know* that the *officers* of the Prussian army serve for longer than the 3 years, I will change *man* to *private*.

If it is as you say the Prussians have a more instructed body of officers than I imagined, but the fact remains as to the 'gros' of their army. And I imagine raw troops only fight well on quite exceptional occasions, such as the national uprising of 1813. Lord Cowley, who has been much in Germany, and was inclined to overrate the Austrians, told me I was quite right about the Prussians: 'The French,' he said, 'would walk over and over and over them in a fortnight'—and Pellissier told the Emperor that with 80,000 men at Nancy he would undertake to dispose of any army the Prussians could bring into France.

I do not wish to depreciate Prussia—I sincerely wish she was stronger (and a little *depedantified* at the same time) but people here all overrate her force, and she can only become strong by being helped and encouraged to absorb the wretched little German states.

The strong point of the pamphlet is, I fairly believe, that it is in the main true—being convinced of the truth of it and having carried it all in my head some weeks, I wrote it with great zest and pleasure. I don't know how it is going on, but I imagine well. I am to hear from the Longmans tomorrow. I had a very warm note from Gladstone about it just before he made his speech. How my great Whig friends take it, I know not—I wrote in the earnest desire to influence them, and to approach them on an accessible side—but they are *very* hard to get at. I should like it to be read by the middle classes who I am told are savagely and blindly anti-Louis-Napoleon-ist—tell Walrond he ought to make Dasent[3] get it reviewed in the Times—without that it will never reach below intelligent London society. They certainly misconceive Louis Napoleon in this country and may end by *misdriving* him—not that he will come to any good if left to himself and treated with all fairness. Still, with fairness let us treat him, and all men and things.

I sent Lowe[4] a copy—has he said anything about it? A horrid thought strikes me that it was *he* who said, at Calne, 'the most unjustifiable war etc.'[5]—but if he *did* say it, he shouldn't have. I saw it in some French newspaper. I am so glad you are with him as his secretary. Let me have a line *here*—I return to Paris for a week or so on Sunday. Kindest regards from us both to your wife—your ever affectionate

M. A.

[1] See his lecture on *The Modern Element in Literature* and *Pagan and Medieval Religious Sentiment.*
[2] The point on which Clough had checked Arnold was: 'But her [Prussia's] army, therefore, is a shadow. In her regular forces she has not a man who has served three full years.' (*England and the Italian Question*, London, 1859, p. 33.)
[3] Sir George Webbe Dasent (1817–96), the Scandinavian scholar, who joined Delane as assistant editor of *The Times* in 1845.
[4] Robert Lowe (afterwards Lord Sherbrooke), Vice-President of the

Education Department, was to have several clashes with Arnold on the question of the Revised Code (see *Letters*, i. 168 ff.).

5 Arnold had written, 'He [Louis Napoleon] knew that when he was accused of undertaking, in behalf of Italian nationality, "the most unjustifiable war ever commenced", he was accused of what would go far to reconcile to him popular feeling in all nations, and to make it forgive his despotism' (*England and the Italian Question*, pp. 32–3).

54

Fox How. Ambleside. Sept[ber] 29/59

My dear Clough

As soon as I heard from you I wrote to Froude urging *him* to do your Plutarch in Fraser,[1] having a fancy to reserve myself for the Edinburgh. I think I might be more useful in the Edinburgh, and I think Reeve[2] would not refuse me an article there—and then I could have my time, without having which I could not satisfy myself, as I write by no means easily, and should like to read through the best part of your translation, without speaking of other translations which I must skim, before reviewing it. But Froude says he is so busy he can do nothing—and adds a long rigmarole about your being so happy and so virtuous that it is not desirable to get literary work out of you—in that regular Carlylean strain which we all know by heart and which the clear-headed among us have so utter a contempt for—since we know very well that so long as *segnities* is, as Spinoza says, with *superbia* the great bane of man, it will need the stimulant of literary work or something equally rousing, to overcome this, and to educe out of a man what virtue there is in him. I for my part find here that I could willingly fish all day and read the newspapers all the evening, and so live—but I am not pleased with the results in myself of even a day or two of such life.

To return to the review of your Plutarch—I incline to wait and see what I can do with Reeve—but if you prefer an article in Fraser, to come earlier, I will, as soon as ever I have done this French Report,[3] see or write to Parker about it.—I think your notion of a selection very judicious—there is no sale for a book like a school sale.

    With our united kindest regards to your wife, believe me,
ever yours
M. ARNOLD.—

I will give you a note to Wm Longman if you like, but it would be better I should speak to him when I come back to London at the end of this month, if that is not too late. I have some time ago talked to him about this Plutarch of yours. He is, as regards books, a thorough *tradesman*, though a capital fellow as regards everything else.

Envelope addressed:
> A. H. Clough Esq.
> Privy Council Office, London.

forwarded
> care of S. Smith Esq.
> Combe Hurst, Kingston, S.W.
> [by] F. R. Sandford.

   ¹ Clough's five-volume edition of Plutarch, published in Boston by Little, Brown & Co., was ready in 1859.
   ² Henry Reeve (1813–95) had been made editor of the *Edinburgh Review* in 1855.
   ³ The report of his study of the schools abroad.

<h2 align="center">55</h2>

[Clough's health, which had never been strong, had begun to fail in 1859. His autumn holiday the following year, although passed in his favourite Scotland, did him no good. He then underwent several weeks of treatment at Malvern.

    As Professor of Poetry at Oxford, Arnold gave, in 1860, his lectures on translating Homer. His chief contention against Francis Newman was that Homer maintained, even though he was rapid and plain and simple, a continued elevation of style; that he was always noble.

    Clough's specimen lines, which Arnold had just examined, have a tendency apparently to Newman's failing—a few notes are 'pitched too low'.]

2, Chester Square [London]
Dec^{ber} 10, 1860

My dear Clough

    I ought to have sent you these back before, but I had to lecture on Saturday, and was hard pressed all last week.

152

As you say the hard thing is to give the requisite elevation without being stilted. The only fault of your lines is, it seems to me, that they do not enough give this—yet this one *must* give, if one is at all to render Homer. 'Greatly disturbed' for μέγ' ὀχθήσας* in the first line seems to me just a specimen of the *pitch a few notes too low* which is the only fault of the whole. The 'eyebrows' line is best, I think, as it stands; the third line from the end seems to me not to scan.

I have done Newman—and now have a third lecture for next term to lay down a little positive doctrine having negatived enough. About the end of January I shall publish the three lectures and will send them to you. I have got off sending them to 'Fraser' as I found three would be enough for an 'opusculum'.

Max Müller got tremendously beaten on Friday[1] which I was very sorry for, but he hurt his own cause. The final adjuration to come up to vote for one 'whose labours had been so precious to the Scholar and the *Missionary*' was too strong for the liberal party, coming from such a quarter, and did him harm. I hope we shall meet at Xmas—we hoped to have got your wife to come and dine here this week, but it seems she is at Hampstead and can't come.

Ever yours
M. A.

[1] Friedrich Max Müller (1823–1900) stood for the Boden Professorship of Sanskrit on December 7, 1860. The election created much excitement and brought special trains to Oxford. Mr. Monier Williams, the rival candidate, was elected.

———

56

[In February 1861, his health still failing, Clough moved to Freshwater in the Isle of Wight, where he enjoyed Tennyson's friendship. Here he resumed his former habit of translating Homer, in the very time of Arnold's interest in it for the Oxford lectures. See the references in these lectures (pp. 213 ff.) to Clough's *Bothie*.

* See *Iliad*, i. 517.

Charles Penrose was Arnold's cousin. For full text of his letter which was enclosed herewith, see Appendix VI.]

[post marked March 9, 1861]
2, Chester Square

My dear Clough

I don't like to leave your letter and translations un-acknowledged—yet I cannot at present examine the latter as attentively as I could wish—I am a good deal out of sorts with an influenza I cannot shake off, and have ear-ache tooth-ache sore throat and lumbago all besetting me at once. ὡς γὰρ ἐπεκλώσαντο θεοὶ δειλοῖσι βρότοισιν ζώειν ἀχνυμένοις.*
however, as a sign of life, I send you a letter I have just received from Charles Penrose—in which I know you will be interested from your remembrance of him. Certainly it shews much of his old vitality and cleverness, which I thought had been extinct. I have not seen him for years. His Cid Extract brings out to my mind just the difference between the ballad manner and Homer's—but his letter and argumentation are not the less interesting because they are not convincing. My ailing condition has thrown me behind with my introduction to my French Report, and I dare say for the next week or so I shall lead the life of a dog. So I will keep your extracts by me, and they shall be my first indulgence when I am out of the printer's paws. Ld. Redesdale[1] has written to me a letter not particularly brilliant (he sends me a rendering of Burn's 'Scots wha hae' into ENGLISH *Sapphics*—but it will give me an opportunity of asking him in my answer for a copy of his metrical lucubrations for you. Tell Tennyson he is the last person on whom I should have dreamed of inflicting a volume of poems—but I have great pleasure in sending him anything of mine that he really wants to see. You need not add that I care for his productions less and less and am convinced both Alfred de Musset and Henri Heine are far more profitable studies, if we are to study contemporaries at all.

* *Iliad*, xxiv. 525–6. 'To live in pain is the lot spun by the gods for miserable men.'

God bless you—pick up again fast—we lead a dog's life, even with health. My kindest regards to your wife—

Your ever affectionate—

Envelope addressed: M. A.

    A. H. Clough, Esq.[re]

      A. J. Cameron's, Esq:[re]

      Freshwater Bay, Isle of Wight—

[1] See *On Translating Homer*, pp. 215 ff.

57

[This is the last letter Arnold wrote to Clough. After the vacation on the Isle of Wight, Clough finally went to Greece and Constantinople, in April 1861. Returning to England in June, he was off once more the following month to the Continent, where he went into Auvergne and the Pyrenees, where for a while he was with the Tennysons. In the fall he went on into Italy with Mrs. Clough.

The present letter was sent to Clough on his return from Constantinople. Arnold is obviously worried about his friend's health.]

                11, Regency Square, Brighton

                      July 5th, 1861

My dear Clough

My letters are sent here and I find them when I come down; but, though yours has been here, I see, a day or two, I am still in time to answer it to London. I got your letter from Constantinople and was very glad to have it—still it did not leave me quite easy about you, nor am I quite easy now. You don't say what is the matter, but it can hardly be anything which would make a life of literary work and chance jobs less trying to you than the work of the office— irksome indeed, but comprehended within regular hours and paying one regularly. The mental harass of an un- certain life must be far more irksome than the ennui of the most monotonous employment. Edward is anxious to give up his inspectorship,[1] and has a substantial reason for this wish in the state of his throat—but I entreat him not to cut himself adrift till he sees some place to run into.—In short your first course appears to me entirely inadmissible: the second may be taken, but the place to be applied for is not yet vacant and I hope you will hold on where you are till it is. All the employments you mention under the head of A may be obtained while you hold your present employment—and, when you have obtained one of them, it will be time enough to resign.

I don't think Auvergne² is worth going to except for a geologist—the mountain country of the Hanli Loui, about Puy, I would much rather go to. Why not try Brittany? easy of access, cheap, a climate that would suit you (as cold as England) and deeply interesting. The inns are not good—but there are very fair ones at the chief places, from which one may make excursions.

I told Longman to send you my book³—I think to Kensington, so you will find it when you get home. I shall like you to read it—the introduction particularly. As a true account of the subject it treats of, the book I am sure will stand—in this respect the testimonies I get from France give me very great pleasure—for the philosophy and general considerations were sure to be just to the taste of Frenchmen, but about facts they are particular, when they are facts under their own knowledge. Old Rapet, a severe old fellow, who Guizot says knows more of the subject than any one else in France, writes me—'Si, après avoir passé quelque temps en Angleterre pour étudier l'organisation de son système d'éducation, je venais à publier le résultat de mes études, je m'estimerais trop heureux que mon travail eût la même valeur que le vôtre, et *surtout qu'il reproduisît les faits avec la même exactitude.*' That is the sort of testimony I like. Have you seen Newman's pamphlet⁴ in answer to my lectures. The one impression it leaves with me is of sorrow that he should be so much annoyed. About Spedding⁵ there is much to be said —his great fault is that he is not *ondoyant* and *divers* enough[,] to use Montaigne's language, to deal rightly with matters of poetical criticism.⁶

Kindest regards to your wife. yours affectionately

M. A.—

Envelope addressed:
   A. H. Clough, Esq:ʳᵉ
      21, Campden Hill Road
         Kensington, S.W.

[1] Edward Arnold, Matthew's brother, was also in the Education Department.

[2] In 1855, however, Arnold had urged his sister, Mrs. Forster: 'Go to Auvergne by all means. You say in N. Italy you seemed to perceive where I had got my poetry, but, if you have fine weather, you will perceive it yet more in Auvergne.' And he goes on to praise it. (*Letters*, i. 53.)

[3] *Popular Education in France* appeared in 1861. Rapet had been very kind in assisting Arnold.

[4] Francis Newman had replied to Arnold's criticism somewhat angrily, in *Homeric Translation in Theory and Practice*, included in the Oxford Standard Authors edition of Arnold's *Essays*.

[5] For Spedding's translations and Arnold's opinion, see *Last Words on Translating Homer*.

[6] 'The critic of poetry should have the finest tact, the nicest moderation, the most free, flexible, and elastic spirit imaginable; he should be indeed the 'ondoyant et divers', the *undulating and diverse* being of Montaigne'. (*Last Words on Homer*, p. 245.)

On November 13, 1861, Arthur Clough died at Florence and was buried there in the Protestant Cemetery outside the walls.

Seven days later Arnold wrote to his mother: 'First of all, you will expect me to say something about poor Clough. That is a loss which I shall feel more and more as time goes on, for he is one of the few people who ever made a deep impression upon me, and as time goes on, and one finds no one else who makes such an impression, one's feeling about those who did make it gets to be something more and more distinct and unique. Besides, the object of it no longer survives to wear it out himself by becoming ordinary and different from what he was. People were beginning to say about Clough that he never would do anything now, and, in short, to pass him over. I foresee that there will now be a change, and attention will be fixed on what there was of extraordinary promise and interest in him when young, and of unique and imposing even as he grew older without fulfilling people's expectations. I have been asked to write a Memoir of him for the *Daily News*, but that I cannot do. I could not write about him in a newspaper now, nor can, I think, at length in a review, but I shall some day in some

way or other relieve myself of what I think about him.'
Letters, i. 176–7.

But at Oxford, in his last lecture on Homer, delivered the Saturday before the following letter was sent to Mrs. Clough, Arnold had paid a considerable tribute:

'And how, then, can I help being reminded what a student of this sort we have just lost in Mr. Clough, whose name I have already mentioned in these lectures? He, too, was busy with Homer; but it is not on that account that I now speak of him. Nor do I speak of him in order to call attention to his qualities and powers in general, admirable as these were. I mention him because, in so eminent a degree, he possessed these two invaluable literary qualities, —a true sense for his object of study, and a single-hearted care for it. He had both; but he had the second even more eminently than the first. He greatly developed the first through means of the second. In the study of art, poetry, or philosophy, he had the most undivided and disinterested love for his object in itself, the greatest aversion to mixing up with it anything accidental or personal. His interest was in literature itself; and it was this which gave so rare a stamp to his character, which kept him so free from all taint of littleness. In the saturnalia of ignoble personal passions, of which the struggle for literary success, in old or crowded communities, offers so sad a spectacle, he never mingled. He had not yet traduced his friends, nor flattered his enemies, nor disparaged what he admired, nor praised what he despised. Those who knew him well had the conviction that, even with time, these literary arts would never be his. His poem, of which I before spoke, has some admirable Homeric qualities;—out-of-doors freshness, life, naturalness, buoyant rapidity. Some of the expressions in that poem,—'*Dangerous Corrievreckan. . . . Where roads are unknown to Loch Nevish,*'—come back now to my ear with the true Homeric ring. But that in him of which I think oftenest is the Homeric simplicity of his literary life.' *Last Words, etc.*, pp. 299–300.

The five letters to Mrs. Clough that follow are themselves quite clear.

58

2, Chester Squa
Dec^{ber}

My dear Mrs. Clough

This will not reach you till your return hon
some delay, I received Miss Clough's letter only a day or
two ago, and was afraid, if I wrote to Florence, that my
letter might not get there until after you had left it.

Slight as your acquaintance with me has been, and much
as circumstances have in the last few years separated me
from him, you will not doubt that few can have received
such a shock in hearing of his death as I did. Probably you
hardly know how very intimate we once were; our friendship was, from my age at the time when it was closest,
more important to me than it was to him, and no one will
ever again be to me what he was. I shall always think—
although I am not sure that he would have thought this
himself,—that no one ever appreciated him—no one of his
men friends, that is—so thoroughly as I did; with no one of
them was the conviction of his truly great and profound
qualities so entirely independent of any visible success in
life which he might achieve. I had accustomed myself to
think that no success of this kind, at all worthy of his great
powers, would he now achieve—and, after all, this would
only have been common to him with one or two other men
the influence of whose works is most precious to me—but
now his early death seems to have reopened all the possi-
bilities for him, and I think of him again as my father
thought of him and as we all thought of him in the extra-
ordinary opening of his youth, as not only able but likely
to have been as profoundly impressive and interesting to
the world as he was to us. Alas, who else of us had freshness and depth enough left for his friends to have been able
to feel thus of him, dying at 42?

You will let me know when I may come and see you:
believe me that I shall always have the strongest interest
in you and in his children.   Most sincerely yours

MATTHEW ARNOLD.—

I shall be most anxious to know what is done about the

unpublished things he has left. I could not yet write about him for the newspapers: but I said a few words in a lecture at Oxford on Saturday.

———————

59

Chester Square [London]
Jany 22 nd, 1862

My dear Mrs. Clough

I cannot tell you how glad I am to have the lines you have sent me. I shall take them with me to Oxford, where I shall go alone after Eáster;—and there, among the Cumner hills where we have so often rambled, I shall be able to think him over as I could wish. Here, all impressions are half impressions, and every thought is interrupted.

I shall have the greatest possible interest in seeing you again, and will most gladly come down on Sunday afternoon—but I must return by the last train if possible.

Believe me,
Ever most sincerely yours
MATTHEW ARNOLD.—

Envelope addressed:
   Mrs. Clough
    Combe Hurst
    Kingston
      S.W.

———————

60

Harrow. Oct ber 2, 1868.

My dear Mrs. Clough

I do not like to refuse any request of yours about your dear husband, but I feel so disinclined to the task of attempting anything like a set memoir of him, or of any part of his life, that I am sure I should not do it well. It occurs to me that Professor Shairp might better than any one else write a sketch of the impression your husband made in those unforgettable Oxford days; Shairp was at just the right distance from him, I was somewhat too near; and in his account of Keble, Shairp has shown how deep

and vivid a sense he retains, and can communicate, of
what was most interesting in the Oxford of our day; there
was nothing there more interesting, or which Shairp felt to
be more interesting, than your husband, and I can imagine
no one whose record of him would be more sympathetic
than his, or more attractive and calculated to inspire sympathy. I cannot help thinking, too, that he would like the
task of attempting to make this record, though I have no
authority for saying so.

We have been in much anxiety about our eldest boy[1] who
had at Fox How a fall from his pony to throw his poor
troubled circulation into more trouble still; but he seems
at last to be slowly coming round.

Believe me, my dear Mrs. Clough,
> ever very sincerely yours
> MATTHEW ARNOLD.—

Envelope addressed:
Mrs. Clough
Holloway House
Old London Road
Hastings

[1] Thomas, aged sixteen, who died at Harrow, November 23, 1868.

61

Harrow. Oct^{ber} 14th. 1868.

My dear Mrs. Clough

I find your letter here on my return home after a short
absence, and write one line in answer before I start for a
second. I am quite sure I should neither satisfy you nor
myself if I tried to throw into form for publication my
recollections of your husband; and on the special point you
mention—his resignation of his fellowship—I could say
nothing; for I had already left Oxford and had ceased to
be in continual communication with him, when it happened.
It was a subject, too, on which he was not likely to have
been communicative to any one. On this and many other
such points he expressed himself in his poems with more
ease and unreserve than in his conversation; and his poems,
to my mind, rather enlarge the communication he made of

himself, than are capable of having what they tell of him enlarged by the report of friends. Shairp could probably write a few charming pages about him—but beyond these, and what Palgrave has already done, I should be inclined to let his letters and poems tell their own story.

Believe me,
ever sincerely yours,

Envelope addressed: MATTHEW ARNOLD.—
  Mrs. Clough
    Holloway House
      Hastings

62

Harrow. Nov^{ber} 29th, 1868.

My dear Mrs. Clough

I should in any case have felt your kindness in writing to me in our great loss,[1] and to hear from the wife of your dear husband can never seem to me anything but natural. I remember his expressing interest in my poor darling and his pale face. I suppose every one, but his mother and I, thought that he could not live to grow up—but we had seen him spared so often when he was threatened, that we went on day after day and hoped he would be spared still. We took him yesterday to Laleham where my father lived when he was first married, and laid him in the churchyard there by his poor little brother.[2] Mrs. Arnold got through the long endless day better than I could have hoped.

I should very much like to see you and your children some time in the course of this next year, and will try and effect it.

Believe me, dear Mrs. Clough,
gratefully and sincerely yours,

Envelope addressed: MATTHEW ARNOLD.——
  Mrs. Clough
    Combe Hurst
      Kingston
        S.W.

[1] The death of his eldest son (see p. 161, note 1).
[2] Basil, who had died on January 4 of the same year.

[This collection of letters may be perhaps best closed by a quotation from a letter Matthew Arnold wrote to a friend at the time of Clough's death. The friend had cut off the post-script and forwarded it to Mrs. Clough:]

P. S. Stanley will, I hope, draw up a short notice of Clough. I cannot say his death took me altogether by surprise—I had long had a foreboding something was deeply wrong with him. But the impression he left was one of those which deepen with time and such as I never expect again to experience.

APPENDIX I

The Origin of 'Rugby Chapel'.

In a letter to his mother of August 8, 1867, which I publish here by the kindness of Mrs. Florence Vere O'Brien, Arnold says:

'I knew, my dearest mother, that the Rugby Chapel Poem would give you pleasure: often and often it had been in my mind to say it to you, and I have foreborn because my own saying of my things does not please me. It was Fitzjames Stephen's thesis, maintained in the Edinburgh Review, of Papa's being a narrow bustling fanatic, which moved me first to the poem. I think I have done something to fix the true legend about Papa, as those who knew him best feel it ought to run: and this is much——.'

The review of *Tom Brown's School-days* in the *Edinburgh Review*, cvii (1858), pp. 172–93, is assigned to Fitzjames Stephen by his brother, Leslie Stephen, in his *Life of Sir James Fitzjames Stephen*, 1895, p. 484. What the review stresses is Dr. Arnold's so-called want of humour, which led the Rugby boy to the point where 'he never ties his shoes without asserting a principle; when he puts on his hat he "founds himself" on an eternal truth'; where praepostor's penny canes were turned into 'the sword of the Lord and of Gideon'.

A critic such as Sainte-Beuve would enjoy knowing that Sir James Stephen had been told as a lad that Dr. Arnold could read a boy's character at one glance. 'At Easter 1841, my father', Leslie Stephen tells us, 'took his boy to see the great schoolmaster at Rugby. Fitzjames draws a little diagram to show how distinctly he remembers the scene. He looked at the dark, grave man and wondered, '"Is he now reading my character at a glance?"' He entered Eton! *Life of James Fitzjames Stephen*, p. 76.

APPENDIX II

A letter from A. P. Stanley to Arthur Clough, written upon the death of Dr. Thomas Arnold. The manuscript is at present in possession of Mr. A. H. Clough.

[June 1842.]

My dear Clough

Finding from Ward that you are absolutely ignorant of the details, I write to you at once. The furious attack consequent upon the rupture of the marriage had past off, leaving no other traces than a most remarkable gentleness and quiet, of which I had seen the beginning in the extreme tenderness and kindness w[hic]h he had shown to Cotton, and which during the whole of the last month seems to have come out in so absorbing a degree as to have struck every one even before his death, servants, boys, masters—and now of course still more deeply. Lake also who was in the home for the last 3 days felt it the more for his talking to him without harshness rather with the greatest forbearance on the Oxford views etc.— especially on the last evening, when he was in high spirits, but overflowing with this deep tenderness and love.

For the last 3 weeks he had for the first time in his life kept from time to time a Diary of prayers and meditations having said to Mrs. A. that so many good men had done so that it was perhaps a want of humility in him never to have tried anything of the kind. The farewell sermon had been preached the Sunday before, taking a review of his whole school life— the whole of the school business had been wound up on Sat[ur]day afternoon—and before going to bed at 12 P.M. on Saturday night, he wrote the following passage in his Diary, w^h was not found till after his death, and w^h you must not allow any one to copy. 'Saturday even^g. June 11th. The day after tomorrow is my birthday—my 47th birthday since my birth. How large a portion of my life on earth is already past— and then? What is to follow this life?—How visibly my outward work seems contracting and softening away into the gentler employments of old age. In one sense how nearly may I now say " Vixi ".—And I thank God that so far as ambition is concerned it is I trust fully mortified—I have no desire other than to step back from my present place in the world, and not to rise to a higher one. Still there are works w^h with God's permission I w^d perform before the night cometh—

especially that great work, if I am permitted to bear my part in it.—But above all let me mind my own personal work to keep myself pure, and zealous and believing, labouring to do God's will, yet not unwilling that it should be done by others if God disapproves of my doing it.'—at 5½ A.M. on Sunday morning he woke with a slight pain in the chest. W^h gradually increased till Mrs. A. alarmed got up and sent for Bucknill who came at ¼ to 7. The first half hour it seems to have been very great—he lay with his hands clasped,—his eyes upwards, —praying in silence most fervently—Once he said 'Jesus said unto him " Thomas, because thou has seen etc.",' and again a short time afterwards with a depth and solemnity, which told Mrs. A. even more than the words themselves 'If ye be without chastisement etc. etc.'—He then asked her to read Ps. 51. Smiled when she reminded him that the 7th verse was the favourite one of an old almshouse woman whom he had been in the habit of visiting and repeated aloud after her the 12th. To Bucknill he put a vast number of questions as to the disease, which B. soon ascertained and told him the exact truth. My belief is tho' he never said it that he knew that he was dying.—At one of the answers to the questions he said in his peculiar way 'Ah.'—as much as to say I understand it.—When Tom who was called up came to him, he said 'My son, thank God for me.'—'Thank God for having sent me this pain. I never had pain before, and I feel it is good for me, and I am *so* thankful.' Mrs. A. then read to him the Exh. in the Visit. of the Sick and at every sentence he most fervently said 'Yes,'—'Yes.' Mrs. A. had just called Tom out of the room, to tell him, wt. he did not seem aware of,—of his father's great danger—when the scream from the stairs called her up—The fatal paroxysm had come in—the screams of the children who were all brought in produced no impression upon him—a few long sighs—and in three minutes he was gone.—I have no time to write more—but these are the essential points—they give you (what I spoke of) the almost preternatural preparation, the almost royal majesty of his death, wh. if they are not positive illusions, seem to affix the last seal which could be given to his character as being one of the greatest and holiest men whom this generation has produced.

Ever yrs.
A. P. STANLEY.

APPENDIX III

Two excerpts from novels of George Sand (see Letter 2, p. 57).

A

[From *Indiana*, partie xxiii, nouvelle édition, Calmann Lévy, Paris, 1900, pp. 232–5.]

Indiana writes to assure Raymon, who has not understood her passionate love, that he may be sure of her good will. The quotation is from the last part of her letter:

'Soyez heureux, c'est le dernier vœu que formera mon cœur brisé. Ne m'exhortez plus à penser à Dieu; laissez ce soin aux prêtres, qui ont à émouvoir le cœur endurci des coupables. Pour moi, j'ai plus de foi que vous; je ne sers pas le même Dieu, mais je le sers mieux et plus purement. Le vôtre, c'est le dieu des hommes, c'est le roi, le fondateur et l'appui de votre race; le mien, c'est le Dieu de l'univers, le créateur, le soutien et l'espoir de toutes les créatures. Le vôtre a tout fait pour vous seuls; le mien a faites toutes les espèces les unes pour les autres. Vous vous croyez les maîtres du monde; je crois que vous n'en êtes que les tyrans. Vous pensez que Dieu vous protège et vous autorise à usurper l'empire de la terre; moi, je pense qu'il le souffre pour un peu de temps, et qu'un jour viendra où, comme des grains de sable, son souffle vous dispersera. Non, Raymon, vous ne connaissez pas Dieu; ou plutôt laissez-moi vous dire ce que Ralph vous disait un jour au Lagny: c'est que vous ne croyez à rien. Votre éducation, et le besoin que vous avez d'un pouvoir irrécusable pour l'opposer à la brutale puissance du peuple, vous ont fait adopter sans examen les croyances de vos pères; mais le sentiment de l'existence de Dieu n'a point passé jusqu'à votre cœur, jamais peut-être vous ne l'avez prié. Moi, je n'ai qu'une croyance, et la seule sans doute que vous n'ayez pas: je crois en lui; mais la religion que vous avez inventée, je la repousse: toute votre morale, tous vos principes, ce sont les intérêts de votre société que vous avez érigés en lois et que vous prétendez faire émaner de Dieu même, comme vos prêtres ont institué les rites du culte pour établir leur puissance et leur richesse sur les nations. Mais tout cela est mensonge et impiété. Moi qui l'invoque, moi qui le comprends, je sais bien qu'il n'y a rien de commun entre lui et vous, et c'est en m'attachant à lui de toute ma force que je m'isole de vous, qui tendez sans cesse à renverser ses ouvrages et à souiller ses dons. Allez, il vous sied mal d'invoquer son nom pour anéantir la résistance d'une faible femme, pour étouffer la plainte d'un cœur déchiré. Dieu ne veut pas qu'on opprime et qu'on écrase les créatures de ses mains. S'il daignait descendre jusqu'à intervenir dans nos chétifs intérêts, il briserait le fort et relèverait le faible; il passerait sa grande main sur nos têtes inégales et les nivellerait comme les eaux de la mer; il dirait à l'esclave: "Jette ta chaîne, et fuis sur les monts où j'ai mis pour toi des eaux, des fleurs et du soleil." Il dirait aux rois: "Jetez la pourpre aux mendiants pour leur servir de natte, et allez dormir dans les vallées où j'ai étendu pour vous des tapis de mousse et de bruyère." Il dirait aux puissants: "Courbez le genou, et portez le fardeau de vos frères débiles: car désormais vous aurez besoin d'eux, et je leur donnerai la force et le courage." Oui, voilà mes rêves; ils sont tous d'une autre vie, d'un autre monde, où la loi du brutal n'aura point passé sur la tête du pacifique, où du moins la résistance et la fuite ne seront pas des crimes, où l'homme pourra échapper à l'homme, comme la gazelle échappe à la panthère, sans que la chaîne des lois soit tendue autour de lui pour le forcer à venir se jeter sous les pieds de son ennemi, sans que la voix du préjugé s'élève dans sa détresse pour insulter à ses souffrances et lui dire: "Vous serez lâche et vil pour n'avoir pas voulu fléchir et ramper."

'Non, ne me parlez pas de Dieu, vous surtout, Raymon; n'invoquez pas son nom pour m'envoyer en exil et me réduire au silence. En me soumettant, c'est au pouvoir des hommes que je cède. Si j'écoutais la voix que Dieu a mise au fond de mon cœur, et ce noble instinct d'une nature forte et hardie, qui peut-être est la vraie conscience, je fuirais au désert, je saurais me passer d'aide, de protection et d'amour; j'irais vivre pour moi seule au fond de nos belles montagnes; j'oublierais les tyrans, les injustes et les ingrats. Mais, hélas! l'homme ne peut se passer de son semblable, et Ralph lui-même ne peut pas vivre seul.

'Adieu, Raymon! puissiez-vous vivre heureux sans moi! Je vous pardonne le mal que vous me faites. Parlez quelquefois de moi à votre mère, la meilleure femme que j'aie connue. Sachez bien qu'il n'y a contre vous ni dépit ni vengeance dans mon cœur; ma douleur est digne de l'amour que j'eus pour vous.

INDIANA.'

B

[From *Jacques*, partie xxix, nouvelle édition, p. 142.]

Jacques in the 'Sunday-shoes letter' writes Sylvia that Fernande is under the power of conventions.

'. . . On ne lui a pas fait, comme à toi, un corps et une âme de fer; on lui a parlé de prudence, de raison, de certains calculs pour éviter certaines douleurs, et de certaines réflexions pour arriver à un certain bien-être que la société permet aux femmes à de certaines conditions. On ne lui a pas dit comme à toi: "Le soleil est âpre et le vent est rude; l'homme est fait pour braver la tempête sur mer, la femme pour garder les troupeaux sur la montagne brûlante. L'hiver, viennent la neige et la glace, tu iras dans les mêmes lieux, et tu tâcheras de te réchauffer à un feu que tu allumeras avec les branches sèches de la forêt; si tu ne veux pas le faire, tu supporteras le froid comme tu pourras. Voici la montagne, voici la mer, voici le soleil; le soleil brûle, la mer engloutit, la montagne fatigue. Quelquefois les bêtes sauvages emportent les troupeaux et l'enfant qui les garde: tu vivras au milieu de tout cela comme tu pourras; si tu es sage et brave, on te donnera des souliers pour te parer le dimanche."'

APPENDIX IV

Documentation of certain notes to the letters.

For Letter 8, note 2 (p. 69):

Arnold's paragraph on 'the eternal relations between labour and capital *The Times* twaddles so of' was inspired by a leading article that appeared the morning of Wednesday, March 1. The editorial thinks the promise of the new French Government to secure work for the people by national workshops or *ateliers* savours of Louis Blanc's socialistic doctrines, seductive and dangerous to society as a whole. It goes on to say (italics my own):

'The purport of these fallacious promises and engagements is nothing short of a metamorphosis of the world, and a total change *of all the laws which experience and reflection have demonstrated to be the rules which govern human wealth and human labour, and consequently regulate the conditions of mankind.* To fulfill such promises is not only beyond the power of any Government, but absolutely *contrary to the laws of nature itself*, and it may be

169

conjectured what the probable consequences are of making, in a moment of triumph, such promises as these, which are destined by *inevitable necessity* to be turned into the bitterest disappointment hereafter.' (*The Times*, March 1, 1848, p. 5.)

That same day *The Times* carried a letter from Paris (p. 6), expressing fears over the new experiment, and deploring the notion among English workmen that 'their privations and severe labour are caused by the selfishness of their masters'. The remedy suggested is 'the education of the people, especially the diffusing amongst them a knowledge of the *natural causes* which determine the distribution of the products of labour and capital'.

For Letter 12, note 1 (p. 77):

At Manchester on January 25, Richard Cobden made a strong speech against British naval expansion. He said that the American consul at Malta had in conversation with him observed that the Americans considered the British navy very slack in its use of the ships it already had. On Monday, March 20, Admiral Dundas presented in the House of Commons a letter from Vice Admiral Sir Wm. Parker, reporting that the American Consul at Malta had written to declare he had not seen Cobden at Malta for ten years. Cobden replied that it was perfectly true, he *had* been at Malta in the winter of 1836 and the spring of 1837, and that he had been four days on a steamer with the American between Malta and Gibraltar. Then Admiral Dundas read from the report of Cobden's speech, 'I was at Malta at the commencement of winter, in the month of November'; whereupon he himself added, 'Had the hon. gent. said candidly that he spoke of ten years ago I should have understood him'. (*The Times*, Tuesday, March 21, p. 4.)

An editorial of March 21 struck a hard blow at Cobden, saying, 'It will require all the traditions of the Corn-law agitation to keep the hon. member for the West Riding straight with the country.' (*The Times*, Tuesday, March 21, 1848, p. 5.) That Arnold's interpretation of the reaction against Cobden is correct is shown by the severe leading article in *The Times* for Friday, April 7, 1848, p. 4: 'Mr. Cobden, we grieve to say it, has not hesitated at a permutation of facts, and a suppression of the element of time in his narration, utterly unworthy of his former reputation. The evasion that was fixed upon him the other night in the House of Commons by Admiral Dundas . . . will do more to damage Mr. Cobden in the minds of all straightforward men than a hundred political blunders, even were the blunders as great as those committed by Mr. Cobden since his return to England. The Parliamentary report is before the world—let it judge for itself.'

It is interesting to find in a later MS. letter from Clough to Stanley, May 26, 1848, 'How glad I am that Cobden has got (apparently) so well out of that awkward Malta business'. Later in his essay *On the Study of Celtic Literature*, Arnold recalls Mr. Cobden as 'A man of exquisite intelligence and charming character'. (p. 134.)

For Letter 13, note 2 (p. 79):

With the outbreak of the revolutions in other countries, the Russian czar had mustered large forces on the border. The strong Polish sympathy in many parts of England, together with the general mistrust of Russia among certain parties in London, had spurred Mr. Anstey to forward a motion in the House on April 4 for an address to the Queen, asking her not to 'consent to any territorial or other arrangement consequent upon such events that does not recognize and secure to the Polish people their lawful liberties and independence'. He was afraid of some possible artificial alliance even being made with Russia in the general uncertainty of the times. He continued: 'The treaty of Venice had now become impracticable, if not impossible, and the territorial arrangement which was to last till the end of time existed no longer. It would be impossible for Her Majesty to avoid becoming a party to an arrangement with some of the powers of Europe for the purpose of maintaining the minor states against the aggression of the larger, and, without a barrier against the progress of northern ambition, it was impossible that any such arrangement could last. If the danger were near, it was fit that this address should be carried; if it were distant the adoption of it could do no harm. Adopt it, and foreign powers would know that they might safely treat with us, and co-operate with us in the grand common design of driving back Russia to its native barbarism and native snows; but reject it, and still a warning would have gone forth to the nations of which they would not be slow to avail themselves.' *The Times*, Wednesday, April 5, 1848.

The next day, *The Times* reproduced the Manifesto of March 26 of the Russian Emperor, deploring the revolutionary changes prevalent in Europe. It contained also this dithyrambic avowal: 'Faithful to the example handed down from our ancestors, having first invoked the aid of the Omnipotent, we are ready to encounter our enemies from whatever side they may present themselves, and without sparing our own person we will know how, indissolubly united to our holy country, to defend the honour of the Russian name, and the inviolability of our territory. We are convinced that every Russian, that every one of our faithful subjects will respond with joy to the call of his Sovereign. Our ancient war-cry, "For our faith, our Sovereign and our country" will once again lead us on the path of victory, and then with sentiments of humble gratitude, as now with feelings of holy hope, we will cry with one voice "God is on our side, understand this ye people and submit, for God is on our side"'.

Lord Palmerston, then Foreign Secretary, wished to be on good terms with Russia, although he wanted a Constitution for Poland. On April 11, 1848, he wrote to Lord Bloomfield at St. Petersburg: 'Assure Count Nesselrode that our feelings and sentiments towards Russia are exactly similar to those which he expresses to you towards England. We are at present the only two Powers in Europe (excepting always Belgium) that remain standing upright, and we ought to look with confidence to each other. Of course, he must be aware that public feeling in this country runs strong in favour of the Poles; but we, the Government, will never do anything underhand or ungentlemanlike on those matters. I wish we could hope that the Emperor might of his own accord settle the Polish question in some satisfactory manner.' Ashley, *Life of Palmerston*, London, 1876, i. 91–2.

For Letter 16, note 3 (p. 85):

The Times of June 27 said, 'The annals of the whole French Revolution and of European warfare hardly present so terrible an example of civil war raging with unabated violence for at least three days and nights in the heart of a great capital', and it deplored 'the incapacity or treachery of the principal rulers of the nation'.

By this time, the old members of the Provisional Government had lost prestige. The *Examiner* of July 1 (p. 417) expressed the general feeling that the anarchists had been favoured by 'the remissness or the guilty connivance of the Government'. *The Times* of the same day held that Lamartine, by retaining Redru-Rollin and attempting to combine with the radicals, was guilty of 'an act of treason to the party [the Moderates] whose suffrages at the first election had placed him in one of the proudest positions ever filled by a French citizen.' It had previously deplored the 'scandalous lie' of M. Cremieux, Minister of Justice, who had revoked his declared willingness to proceed against M. Louis Blanc for alleged part in the conspiracy of May 15. (*The Times*, June 9, 1848, p. 4.) *The Times* of July 7 finally sang a swan song over the old Provisional Government, tolerated long after it 'was known to be dishonest, treacherous, and incapable', and now to be remembered for a catalogue of disgraces including 'the false financial statements and plunder of the savings banks by Mr. Garnier Pagès'.

APPENDIX V

Arnold's letter of recommendation of Clough for the principalship of the college at Sydney, Australia. (See p. 117.)

London. December 5th 1851.

I have long had the pleasure of intimately knowing Mr. Clough, who was for a number of years under my father at Rugby. There was certainly no one of his pupils of whom my father retained a higher—I doubt whether there was one of whom he retained so high an estimate.

Mr. Clough possesses great knowledge both of ancient and modern literature. He is celebrated at Oxford for his power of imparting instruction in the former: his knowledge of the latter he has of late greatly added to. His ability is of the highest order. But it is especially in respect of his moral qualities, and of the intimate manner in which his intellectual qualities are affected by them, that he is distinguished from the crowd of well informed and amiable men who generally offer themselves for public situations. In patience, in self-control, in disinterestedness, in clearness of mind and dignity of character, Mr. Clough, even as a young man, stood above and apart from other young men. That superiority he has continued to retain.

He has always commanded the interest and respect of those about him, and on such as have approached him more closely he has never failed to exercise a very powerful influence.

At the same time that Mr. Clough's friends cannot but deplore that the services of such a man should be lost here, they are deeply sensible of the signal benefit his ability and character would enable him to render to an educational institution in a new country.

M. ARNOLD.
late Fellow of Oriel College, and
one of H.M. Inspectors of Schools.—

173

APPENDIX VI

[See introductory note to letter 56, p. 154.]

13 Holford Square W.C.

March 5th 1861.

My dear Matt.

Many thanks for your Lectures. I have read them with very great interest and delight. If I were to tell you the points on which I have been specially gratified by them, my letter would indeed be a long one. As it is I have no hope of making it short. In even trying to make it so I must confine myself to things wherein I differ from you.—Once for all, these matters in question detract nothing from my estimate of the good service you have done to the cause of true criticism.

Your general subject is one on which I have thought much and often. I have a strong faith in my own opinion, whether a bigoted faith or not I dare not say. At any rate I so fully believe in my own view, and in your candour, that I am not without the high ambition of making you a proselyte. Hence this letter, which shall be as short as I can make it.

(I) I shall begin by demanding a slight qualification of one of your axioms. I grant that a scholar, who is also a man of poetical feeling is the only competent judge of a translation of Homer. But then this same judge is bound to remember that while the translator has to *satisfy* him, the translator does not write for his benefit. He writes to bring Homer within the reach of *non-scholars* of poetic feeling. The scholar-judge is bound to bear this in mind. He must therefore be indulgent to the translator's endeavour to make his version attractive.

This consideration has a strong bearing on the question of rhyme. It satisfies me that if a translation of Homer can be executed in rhyme without *much* departure from the very words of the original, the gain is so great as to counterbalance the loss.—And I think it can be done with no greater licence than you yourself claim and exercise in your 3rd Lecture.

(II) I do not think that if Homer himself were to come to life again in England he could translate a single book of his Iliad into English Hexameters satisfactorily. There is a sing song and monotony in them which is peculiarly wearying to my ear. To perceive the metre at all you are obliged to quasi-scan them. Observe the ugly stress you have to lay on the 1st syllable of the line. You have made the best of them, I grant, by cutting down the allowance of dactyls. Still I think that any metre

174

which requires or even allows more than quite an occasional dactyl or anapaest, is unsuited to noble poetry, or serious poetry of any kind in the English language.

Compare the specimen you quote of D^r. Maginn's with Gladstone. It is solely the trissyllabic feet which give the horrible jingle to the former. That is to say, the element which D^r. M.'s Homeric ballad has in common with English Hexameters.

I have one more stone to shy at the English Hexameter, which is this. It is almost impossible that any metre not of spontaneous English growth should be natural and straightforward enough to reproduce the characteristics of Homer which you so admirably define.

(III) I think your case against the ballad metre a weak one. I can find no argument on this point which is not drawn from the *abuse*, or *tendencies* of the metre in question. But unless you can prove that the tendencies which you so justly object to are *unavoidable* your whole argument seems to me to fall to the ground. I assert that if I could show you but 5 lines together in the ballad metre more truly Homeric than any passage in English poetry which could be compared with them, they would go far to decide the point. They would counterbalance 5000 lines of trash alleged to prove the objectionable *tendency* of the metre. It would be rather a reductio ad absurdum, if one were to take all the rubbish that may be extant in Greek Hexameters, and to argue therefrom that Homer ought to have written in some other metre.

That which to my mind decides the whole question in favour of the Ballad metre, provided the faults into which some ballad writers have fallen can be avoided, is this. The only passages in English poetry which convey to me the same impression as Homer conveys are portions of old ballads, or recent poems in the ballad metre. There are but few such passages, I grant, and those fragmentary, but this is wholly owing to the fact that no great English poet ever wrote in this metre. In short we have no Homer.

I agree with you as to the wide line between Scott and Homer. But I do not think Scott takes a step from the best ballads towards Homer, but in the opposite direction, and this he does very much in so far as his metre departs from the ballad simplicity. His lines are too irregular and his rhymes too frequent. I think the same objection applies to Gladstone's translations, otherwise admirable. They have not the dignity of the regular 14 syllable.

175

Appendix VI

I will wind up by copying two passages one 14 syll. the other 16 which seem to me as Homeric as anything in English can be. I have not the books here, or could probably find still better. I again submit that the whole question turns upon whether the most Homeric passages in the English language are to be found in the ballad metre or what.—

I am quite ashamed to have inflicted such a long yarn upon you. I will only say in conclusion that I believe the book is a practicable one if attempted on *your* principles but in the ballad metre properly sustained.

Ever your affectionate cousin
C. T. PENROSE.

From Hookham Frere's Translation of the 'Chronicle of the Cid'

'And you, Pero Bermuez, my standard you must bear.
Advance it like a valiant man, comely and fair.
But do not venture forward before I give command.'
Bermuez took the standard: he went and kissed his hand.
The gates were then thrown open, and forth at once they rushed.
The outposts of the Moorish host back to the camp were pushed.
The camp was all in tumult, and there was such a thunder
Of cymbals and of drums as if Earth would cleave in sunder.

'My men, stand here in order, ranged upon a line
Let not a man stir from his place before I give the sign.'
Pero Bermuez heard the word, but he could not refrain
He held the banner in his hand, he gave his horse the rein.
'You see yon foremost squadron there, the thickest of the foes
Noble Cid, God be your aid, for there your standard goes,
Let him that serves and honours it show the duty that he owes.'
Earnestly the Cid cried out 'For heaven's sake, be still.'
Bermuez cried 'I cannot hold.' So eager was his will
He spurred his steed and drove him on amidst the Moorish rout
They strove to win the banner, and compassed him about
Had not his armour been so true they had won either life or
    limb,
Again the Cid cried out 'For heaven's sake succour him'.

The Cid was in the midst, his shout was heard afar,
'I am Ruy Diaz the champion of Bivar.
'Strike among them gentlemen for sweet mercy's sake.'
There where Bermuez fought among the foe they break;

176

Three hundred bannered knights, it was a gallant show,
Three hundred Moors they killed, a man with every blow.
When they wheeled and turned, as many more lay slain,
You might see them raise their lances, and level them again.'

2. From Kinmont Willie—Scott's Minstrelsy

Now word is gone to the bold Buccleugh
 In Branksome hall where that he lay,
That Lord Scroope had ta'en the Kinmont Willie
 Between the hours of night and day.
He has ta'en the table with his hand,
 He has gar'd the red wine spring on hie,
'Now Christ's curse on my head, he said,
 But avenged of Lord Scroope I'll be.
O, is my basnet a widow's curch
 Or my lance a wand of the willow tree,
Or my arm a lady's lily hand
 That an English lord should lightly me?
And have they ta'en him Kinmont Willie
 Against the truce of Border tide,
And forgotten that the bold Buccleugh
 Is warden here on the Scottish side?'

INDEX

The abbreviation 'M.A.' is used to indicate Matthew Arnold; 'A.C.' for Arthur Hugh Clough.

48–9, and see 'America'; his theology, 49–51, and see 'Religion';
deplores philosophical jargon, 49;
his letter on George Sand, 57–9;
his ideas concerning 'capital and
labour', 68–9; attends riots in
Trafalgar Square, 74–5; his
theatre-going in London, 72, 73
n. 1, 74–6; discusses resignation of
A.C.'s fellowship, 76; feels strongly
about Irish problem, 77–8; interest in politics and House of
Commons, 48, 80 *et seq.*; on
Rachel and Jenny Lind, 81, 82
n. 10; troubled over A.C.'s situation, 83–9; on war in Lombardy,
84–6; his letters from Switzerland, 91–3, 109–11; comments on
A.C.'s *Bothie*, 95; publishes '*The
Strayed Reveller*, and Other Poems',
100–4; interest in translating
Homer, 100–1 *n.* 1, 103–5, 152–4;
visits Rugby, 112–13; writes
Memorial Verses at request of
Edward Quillinan, 114–15; marriage, 116, 118, 128; worries about
A.C.'s poor health, 116, 155, 163;
recommends A.C. for post in
Australia, 117, 173; his work as
inspector of schools, 117, 119, 125,
136, 139, 140, 142, 146, 147, 149,
150 *n.* 4; his actions misinter-
preted by A.C., 119, 120, 127 *n.* 4;
a lengthy explanation, 128–31;
the matter concluded, 132, 134–5,
138, 148; publishes poems of 1852,
123 *et seq.*; aided by Froude, 126,
127 *n.* 3, 140–1; in Wales, 137 *et
seq.*; welcomes A.C. home from
America, 137–8; vacation at Fox
How, 140–3; prepares preface for
poems of 1853, 141, 144; inscribes
copy of *Merope* for A.C., 148; his
interest in A.C.'s edition of Plutarch, 151–2; his study of French
schools, 148, 156; his letter on
England and the Italian Question,
148–50; lectures at Oxford on
Homer, 152–4, 158; his tribute on
A.C.'s death, 157 *et seq.*; declines
to write memoir of A.C., 161–2;
his claim upon the future, 51–3.
For his estimates of literary men,
contemporaries, and books, see
names of individual writers, &c.

PUBLICATIONS:
(*Poetry*)
Austerity of Poetry, M.A.'s self-
revelation in, 27; quoted, 40.
Buried Life, The, figure of river in,
35; quoted, 51.
Caution to Poets, A, copied in
letter, 126.
Dover Beach, 32; diction of, 40.
Dream, A, 34.
Emerson's Essays, Written in, 36.
Empedocles on Etna, 49; its fault,
127 *n.* 2, 130; quoted, 52.
'*Empedocles on Etna*, and Other
Poems', published 1852, 123,
124, 126, 134 *n.* 6, 135–6, 137
n. 3, 141 *n.* 2. See also separate
titles.
Epilogue to Lessing's Laocoön, 36, 97
n. 2.
Forsaken Merman, The, 107, 127
n. 3.
Friend, To a, 36, 90, 93 *n.* 2, 101
n. 3.
Future, The, quoted, 34.
Gipsy Child by the Sea-shore, To a,
61, 62 *n.* 2.
Haworth Churchyard, 131 *n.* 3.
Heine's Grave, 36.
Horatian Echo, 94 *n.* 3.
Independent Preacher, To an, quoted,
34.
'Marguerite' poems, 110, 112 *n.* 4.
Memorial Verses, April 1850, 36;
composed at request of Edward
Quillinan, Wordsworth's son-
in-law, 114–15.
Merope, 148.
Morality, A.C.'s opinion of, 127
n. 4.
Mycerinus, Froude's suggestion for,
140; quoted, 34, 40.
New Sirens, The, 104; gloss
furnished for, 105–7.
*Obermann, Stanzas in Memory of the
Author of*, quoted, 110, 111 *n.* 1.
Parting, from 'Switzerland', 110,
112 *n.* 4.
'Poems' of 1853, Froude's advice
about, 136, 137 *n.* 3, 140–1. See
also 'Preface to Poems of 1853'
and separate titles.
Rachel, quoted, 40.
Religious Isolation, 62 *n.* 2.
Republican Friend, To a (A.C.), 67.